NEW GOALS FOR OLD AGE

NEW GOALS FOR OLD AGE

Edited by

GEORGE LAWTON

New York : Morningside Heights
COLUMBIA UNIVERSITY PRESS
1943

COLUMBIA UNIVERSITY PRESS, NEW YORK

FOREIGN AGENT: OXFORD UNIVERSITY PRESS, Humphrey Milford, Amen House, London E.C. 4, England, AND B. I. Building, Nicol Road, Bombay, India

Manufactured in the United States of America

PROLOGUE

THE PAPERS gathered together in this volume represent a plot involving fourteen conspirators and having as its purpose bringing grandfather home. Thereby hangs a tale.

Once upon a time in Asia Minor, it was the custom for people who had reached the age of sixty to be taken away to a cave. There they might live in peace the rest of their lives, and, of course, would be out of peoples' way.

It was considered most proper that when the time came for a man to leave for the cave, his son should contribute the necessary food and "chull," a goat-haired woven blanket.

One day a middle-aged man asked his own little boy to take the chull and come with him and grandpa, for they were taking the latter to the cave from which none returned. Though the grandson was brokenhearted at his grandfather's departure, he was about to shoulder the chull obediently when suddenly he was struck by an idea. Cutting the chull in half, he took one part with him and left the other part at home. When the grandfather had been deposited with due filial piety in the cave, son and grandson returned home.

Then it was that the son discovered what had happened to the chull. He scolded the boy severely. "Look what you've done. Everyone would say we were too stingy to give grandpa the whole blanket!" "No, father" the boy replied, "I wasn't being stingy, but I thought it was better to give grandpa only half. . . . Then I could keep the other half for you." The father was terribly shocked to hear this and he began to weep bitterly. When he recovered himself he announced, "Come on, let's return to the cave and bring grandfather home."

And from that time on in Asia Minor no grandfather ever was sent away, and no grandfather was any more in peoples' way.

While medical science is making it easier for people to grow old, the cultural pattern is making it more difficult. It has just begun to dawn upon public consciousness that there are a great many more old people than ever before. Today we have nine million people in this country over sixty-five years of age. In 1980 there will be twenty-six million. We have come to realize that the increasing number of old people in our midst represents a problem. But to the *people* who grow old, to their difficulties as individual men and women—to such matters we have not as yet begun to pay any particular attention.

We feel that it is important to study young people. We see the necessity for the young plant's receiving proper care, but we have much less interest in the period of harvest. Older people are neglected and left to get along as best they can. We forget that they too need assistance. If it is important to give the human animal a good start in life, it is just as important to see that he makes a good finish. We should be as much interested in actual fulfillment as in setting the stage for the realization of possibilities.

Old people have resources for living and for making useful contributions to society which are almost completely untapped today. We have put grandfather in a cave and, lest we go there ourselves in our old age, we should bring him home. What we need is a second declaration of independence to the effect that people still have a right to the pursuit of happiness no matter how old they become.

Old people themselves want to be different. Most of them dislike the conventional picture of crabbed decline as much as younger age groups do. Take the example of Mrs. Thomas, who had just become a member of an old age home, along with two or three other men and women. The new entrants appointed this woman as their spokesman to acknowledge the address of welcome made at an evening gathering of the entire membership of the home. Mrs. Thomas brought her brief reply to a close with this remark: "We want to be sweet apples in this house; not dry, not wormy, not sour."

The conspiratorial collection of papers found in the following pages aims to set down some of the more recent ideas concerning the nature and needs of older people. We have hoped we can contribute something to a changed point of view, which in turn will increase the facilities made available to the aged by the community.

I don't think we can yet boast that we have brought grandfather all the way home. He is still on the road—somewhere between the cave and the dwelling he will know in the world of tomorrow. At any rate, here in this volume we hope are a few of the strategies and maneuvers necessary if we are to get him back. A point of view is prevalent which insists on making the cave safer and cozier—the gilded-cage idea. We don't believe in this. We want grandfather home, part of society, part of the main current of living; suffering and struggling with the rest of us.

These papers were delivered originally in a course, "Mental Health in Old Age," conducted under the auspices of the Section on the Care of the Aged of the Welfare Council of New York City during the year 1940–1941. The audience was made up of persons directly connected with the care of older people, such as superintendents and staff members of old age homes, as well as social workers connected with private agencies and with what was then the Division of Old Age Assistance of the Department of Welfare. Hence we sought to make the lectures as practical as possible and tried to offer a wide sampling of viewpoints. As far as we know, this was among the first * instructional courses in this country to deal with the mental aspects of old age and to attempt to cover the field systematically and bring to bear upon its practical problems the experience of a large number of specialists.

Gibbon said that as we get older we all become more aware of our position in history. Since this is an undertaking which may have its footnote in some future chronicle devoted to the care of the aged, certain acknowledgments must be made.

First to be thanked are the contributors to the volume who took the time and labor to prepare helpful and interesting presentations.

* In 1937, from March 31 to May 5, a series of weekly lectures on "Mental Hygiene in Old Age" was offered by the New York City Committee on Mental Hygiene. This was a real trail-blazing venture. Later that year, the Family Welfare Association of America published these papers in a pamphlet entitled, *Mental Hygiene in Old Age*.

Next I must thank the members of the program committee for their valuable suggestions and coöperation. Without the help of this committee the course would have been impossible. The names to be enscrolled are:

Mrs. Leslie C. Schwartz, Chairman
Mrs. Helen H. Brunot
Mrs. Frederick E. Donaldson
Miss Marian McBee
Mrs. Charles Perkins
Miss Ollie A. Randall
Mrs. Lois T. Schneider

I cannot conclude these acknowledgments without thanking Mrs. Alice Flexner Rothblatt, at the time Secretary of the Section on Care of the Aged, whose efficient management and constant stimulation was of such great assistance to us. Nor can I forget the valuable guidance and encouragement of Robert P. Lane, Executive Director of the Welfare Council.

I also want to thank, for the program committee, the New York School of Social Work for making it possible for us to meet in a convenient location; and to thank Dr. John H. Travis for permission to quote from a private communication of his to the editor.

For permission to quote from works published by them, acknowledgment is made to the following: the American Psychological Association for Harvey C. Lehman and W. S. Gamertsfelder, *Man's Creative Years in Philosophy;* the *Library Journal* for the entire paper by Alice I. Bryan; *Mental Hygiene* for a portion of a paper by Dr. Nolan D. C. Lewis; the National Conference of Social Work for a paper by Mrs. Florence W. Switton delivered at its 1938 meeting; the Science Press for Harry Da Silva's "Age and Highway Accident" in the *Scientific Monthly*, and for Harvey C. Lehman's "The Creative Years: Medicine, Surgery, and Certain Related Fields," also in the *Scientific Monthly;* the Williams and Wilkins Company for Cowdry's *Problems of Ageing* (passages from the chapters of John Dewey and Walter R. Miles).

My special gratitude is due to "A Woman of Seventy-five," the most inspiring and charming of guinea pigs and auditors, for writing the final chapter to order, but that some day will make another book. Above all, I must indicate my appreciation to the superintendents of the homes who were good enough to lend the lecture group their stenographers for the successive afternoons. Only in this way was it possible to obtain a record of many of the lectures and all of the discussion periods. Without their help, this introduction is as far as the "book" would have got.

GEORGE LAWTON

New York City
May, 1943

CONTENTS

NEW GOALS FOR OLD AGE

ADJUSTMENT OVER THE LIFE SPAN

By Lawson G. Lowrey *

EVOLUTION is at work in all living organisms. Life processes are continuous. Old age is not something new that suddenly develops out of a clear sky; it is the culmination of a process which has been going on since long before the birth of the individual. Birth as a phenomenon is merely a point in the life cycle.

Take the matter of physical growth as an example. From the time the egg is fertilized to the time it reaches full development the increase in weight is 11,000,000 times, whereas the increase of weight from the time of birth to average adult maturity is only about 22 times. The living organism during its first nine prenatal months already has exhausted over 99 percent of its capacity for growth. The part we think of as life has to draw upon something less than one percent of the vital potentialities with which this living organism was endowed.

If the physiological processes of life are continous, so are the processes of mental life. The author of a recent article tried to make the point that we might get further with our knowledge of life if we thought of consciousness as a state not of being awake but of being aware. Mental activity still goes on in those interruptions of the conscious waking state which we call sleep, even in the extremely deep sleep which seems the one thing to interrupt the continuity of mental life, the one thing to suspend all intellectual activity.

Working against the continuity of physical and mental life are various types of disintegration. If the process of *evolution* is continuous, so is that of *involution*. The continuance of the life processes is complicated at all times by a growth-limiting tendency, a tend-

* Director, Brooklyn Child Guidance Clinic; Psychiatrist, Brooklyn Hebrew Orphan Asylum; Editor, *American Journal of Orthopsychiatry*.

ency we call senescence or old age. In any individual who lives long enough there is quite likely to come about, for a variety of reasons, some disintegration which will interfere with the smooth continuation of middle life. There are certain episodic waves in the presenile period which seem to me to be all important with reference to what the psychology of the older person will be.

For the individual, at any given moment or point, is the product of all that has gone before; a product, not a simple sum, of the series of environmental factors and stimuli to which he has been exposed and has had to react. It is remarkable that, being exposed to these, he in turn reduces them to their social components.

PERIOD OF INFANCY

While the prenatal period has important bearings on the psychology and physiology of the individual, we will skip a discussion of this period and start with infancy. The chief characteristics of the first few years of life are dependency and the feeling of being "all-powerful" which results. In a sense, our second childhood seventy or eighty years later is a return to this period of omnipotence or all-powerfulness. Infancy offers a great deal of satisfaction, and we all contain within ourselves a great need to return to it. Hence, we can easily find distinctive types of regressive behavior in children, adults, and seniles. It has been possible, through technical therapeutic means, to reconstruct the period of infancy and show that the behavior labeled "regressive" is actually a resumption of infancy's search for pleasure and desire to be omnipotent. The latter desire is based on the fact that the individual, being helpless and unable to do things himself, is able to get others to do them for him: be fed, have his toilet needs attended to, and so forth.

Within this period of infancy, the personality begins to acquire certain definite social behavior trends. Training in eating and toilet habits are matters largely of imposed social control. Now for the first time the child enters into situations where there is conflict. The problem of weaning a baby from breast to bottle, from spoon to cup, is one in which certain powerful forces represented by adult human beings attempt to divert the baby's attention and capacity for appreciation from certain pleasures and try to get him to accept behavior and discipline unpleasant and unwelcome.

The period of omnipotence gradually leads into another period where the individual seriously comes to grips with his environment. In this next stage, the child learns a great deal. In fact, during the first three or four years of a child's life it learns hundreds of times as much as it does during the balance of its life. It learns how to talk, how to walk, and so forth. Many patterns for continuing contact with life, particularly in terms of material accomplishments, are established during these early years. The stretch between the third and fifth birthdays is very important for the individual because for the first time he becomes independent. Another child may be born into the family at this time, which also makes a difference. Owing to unduly marked or sharp repressions by the environment, it may be a time also when the child develops a great deal of unhappiness. This will determine many of the ways in which the individual will react or fail to react to crucial situations in later life.

SCHOOL PERIOD

School is the first great social venture, the time when the individual begins to leave the family unit for a larger arena. In one way or another school is supposed to be a preparation for a vocation which will permit the individual to be economically self-sustaining, this vocation to bear some relationship to either his interest or capacities or both. This particular era in the child's life might be called the period of competitions. These school competitions are far more numerous and intense, and involve many more people than anything which has gone before. They are found in the intellectual, emotional, physical, and athletic areas. The comparisons and rivalries which the child experiences in school for the first time are with children who are of about the same age, size, degree of beauty, and so forth. A little later in this life epoch the boy or girl becomes aware that he has a status in relation to the opposite sex, and this is still another type of competition which he must learn to handle along with those previously mentioned.

School competitions are extraordinarily important in determining the nature of the individual's attitude toward himself and others. They may emphasize the individual's feelings of difference from the group, which then become crystallized in the attitude known as "inferiority complex." If failures in competition, love, and intellectual strivings occur, and if the individual loses the feeling of belonging, of being secure in the group and of actually being accepted by it, there is danger that he will not be able to solve the problems of adult life. Such an individual, carrying about with him an inescapable sense of inadequacy, will have difficulties in making adjustments and will have an unsuccessful, unhappy life. Some day we may agree that the most important function of the teacher is not what she does by way of formal instruction but rather what she does to promote the child's adjustment, since under ordinary circumstances she is the first adult outside the family circle who tends to stand as a parent in relation to the child and as a link between home and the outside world.

ADOLESCENCE

Adolescence might be called the period of "social maturity with a question mark." Into the teen years, with their storm and strife, the individual brings all those habits, reactions, and responses which he has developed previously. Most discussions of adolescence make the term apply to puberty alone rather than to the whole process of sexual ripening. Puberty, I believe, is a stage which is fairly short. For the girl, it is established when she begins regular menstrual periods. In the life of a boy, there is no sharp limitation of the period of adolescence to this one phenomenon of sexual maturation. From two or three years prior to the onset of specific pubertal changes, there are processes which seem to be part and parcel of the adolescent period and these continue to run for four or more years after puberty is definitely established.

If we think of emotional maturity as a period in which the individual has a certain poise, can adapt himself to the pleasant as well as the unpleasant without too much elation or hilarity, has a certain self-control or restraint, and is able to accept present privation in the expectation of future satisfaction, then the emotionally mature person is one who has passed far beyond the period of adolescence. Rarely is emotional maturity to be found before the age of thirty and I know persons of sixty-five and seventy who have never yet achieved it.

Adolescence, considered psychologically, is a time of great idealism. The crusading spirit is found more often during the teen years than in any other period until after middle age. The adolescent's uncertainty of his present position in the world, and his lack of knowledge as to where he wants to go are related to the mixed-up feelings that come with the ripening of the sexual apparatus and the increased intensity of sex desires.

To the adolescent, it is most important that he become a definite part of a group outside of his own family. That is one area of conflict. The second is the unceasing war which the adolescent carries on with the older generation. Finally, the adolescent is undecided about his sexual goal. Out of this last and most important zone of conflict there should emerge a person whose sexual objective is an individual of the opposite sex outside of his own family group.

We must admit that the emancipation of the adolescent from his family involves painful and difficult situations for both child and parent. Here and there we may see an example of a new breed of parents who try to treat their children not as inferiors, but as equals with whom they can share their enjoyment of things. However, it is rare to find a family which possesses so much internal unity that the parents approach the children on an equal footing. If we are honest, we must admit that there is often a wall between parents and children, and that many older people are afraid of their children. Most parents will admit that when their children were babies the adults enjoyed something which they had never had before. They were placed on a pedestal as adored ones who could do no wrong. But the parent inevitably steps down (or is he thrown off?). There comes a time when jealousy develops between child and parent. There is the jealousy which the father feels when the child absorbs so much of the mother's time and interest. I am impressed by the fact that within my own range of experience I have been able to recognize open display of the fact that many parents do not like their children and that this fact is much more in evidence today than twenty years ago. Only recently I have encountered three of the most desperate cases of open hostility between child and parent that I have ever seen. We must bear in mind that there is a conflict in interest between the child and parent. Older people should retain a youthfulness of spirit and adaptability, though it may be difficult for them to do so as they are inclined to be more rigid and "set" in their ways. Most of the rigidity encountered in these people is a defense reaction. It may be very complex, but on the other hand it may be surprisingly simple to penetrate the rigidity and see what kind of person is underneath.

PERIOD OF SOCIAL MATURITY

This is the period in which the individual establishes himself intellectually, vocationally, and socially, in terms of his own individual strivings and in various other ways. On the way to this end there are all sorts of pitfalls and obstacles. Somewhere during this epoch of the life span the individual who functions chiefly in the intellectual area should reach the height of his intellectual powers.

This period of social maturity and that of middle age (forty to sixty) overlap. Somewhere in this age range involution begins. A physician recognizes that there are certain specific disorders associated with the aging person. The fifth and sixth decades of life lead to the seventh, one in which senescent processes are either marked or accelerated, or where declining functions, having reached a certain level, change very little.

PERIOD OF INVOLUTION

Just as we have a definite criterion for the establishment of puberty in women, so is the period of involution, a decided and difficult one for them, definitely marked off. You can see anxiety and repressions coming to the surface at this time. Men do not reveal such a sharp index to the involution period, but certain changes do occur. One point in the psychology of this period might be stressed. Gradually or acutely there may come the realization that it is not safe to leave something over to another year, simply because there may not be so many years. Another point is the forced acknowledgment by the individual himself that he is slipping. There is the realization by the aging man or woman that a new generation is coming along and taking over many things which he has grown to regard during the years as his prerogatives.

Every person who comes into the period of life when for one reason or another he is no longer able to carry on vocationally as well as he once did has something that he has always wanted to do but never got around to doing. If he could now have the opportunity to do that particular thing, he would be happy—at least, so he thinks. This might cover any number of leisure-time activities, small occupations, or skill acquisitions. We should strive constantly to find out what older persons like and want to do, what would be interesting to them. In the course of making this exploration, the investigator is bound to get all sorts of revealing insights. Oftentimes the person who is crotchety in old age is so because of an environmental background factor which may go far back.

We all believe that people ought to grow old gracefully. But children don't grow up gracefully. For instance, consider the feelings of anxiety shown by the girl whose breasts are growing larger and by the boy who realizes for the first time that he will have to shave. We know that people do not pass from childhood to adulthood easily. Most of us manage to reach adulthood, but occasionally someone gets stuck at the childhood or adolescent stage and stays there for the next fifty or sixty years. Just as it is difficult to go from childhood to adulthood easily, so it is difficult to go from late maturity to old age, though the chances are that if a child grew up gracefully, he will grow old gracefully, and therefore it is always helpful to find out how the old person grew as a child. Indeed, we must know a person's past in order to understand and deal most effectively with his present. However, since it is not always possible to delve exhaustively into a person's life history, it is important to develop techniques and devices for dealing, if only superficially, and entirely in terms of the present situation, with those difficulties of older people which arise in daily relationships.

From a discussion of the changes associated with growing old, one passes to the problems of old age. And since my chapter is only an introductory one, this is where I shall stop. The point to remember is that the aging process is continuous and that it carries over from one period to another all that has gone before. According to George Lawton, "Our life span is divided into periods, each with its own problems of adjustment. These age periods are related, not in surface story since the problems change; it is the method of attacking these problems which is likely to remain the same. Throughout the life span, people develop techniques of handling each of their difficulties. Some of these techniques are suitable and efficient, others are inappropriate and wasteful, or a method may be suitable for one age period and not another."

From infancy and childhood we gradually pass to middle age. If we have achieved social and emotional maturity, we will go on to old age with a serenity which will permit us to be "sweet apples," as the Editor states in his Prologue. But if we reach old age without having achieved this maturity—— However, I leave the sour apple aspects to the authors of succeeding chapters.

AGING MENTAL ABILITIES AND THEIR PRESERVATION

By George Lawton *

CHARLOTTE BUHLER, in her volume, *The Course of Human Life as a Psychological Problem,* presents two very interesting charts. One she calls the biological life curve, and in this she tries to show, using several hundred life histories for material, just when we reach the height of our physical powers. Dr. Buhler also presents a biographical life curve, dealing with various aspects of our existence over its entire span. Here an attempt is made to determine at which age human life reaches its greatest amplitude or peak in the following areas: vocational (industrial, artistic, scientific); love, marriage, children; in the satisfaction we get from children, friends, religion.

The work of Dr. Buhler prompts the observation that the person who could find a way of slowing up the descent in any area of human activity would be discovering a fountain of youth, a kind of earthly immortality. What everyone wants, after all, is a larger increment of maturity, a longer period in which he can enjoy the sense of being physically, socially, and mentally effective; we want an additional opportunity for enjoying the privileges, the pleasures, and the profound emotional experiences of adulthood. The older we become, the keener is our sense that the best we can hope for in connection with the final sentence is a reprieve.

However, the extreme limits to our hopes in this direction is something we do not know today. Among the many factors which have hindered our knowledge of old age is the fact that in previous generations a relatively small percentage of the population reached an age we would consider old. In Greek times, the average age at

* Director, Old Age Counselling Center, New York City; formerly Psychological Consultant, Andrew Freedman Home, New York.

death was 29.4 years. In Massachusetts, around 1800, it was 35 years; in 1890, it had risen to 43. The year 1935 saw life expectancy go to 59.3 for males and 62.8 for females. Today it is even slightly higher. With those over 65 now reaching the grand total of 9,000,000 in the United States, we finally have a large enough group to offer at least the opportunity for arriving at valid conclusions regarding old age.

There is one question that is particularly interesting in connection with the matter of life's duration, though the answer is not likely to be soon forthcoming. Are all of us at birth destined to have the same experiences (assuming non-accidental deaths), some to compress them into a shorter life span, others into a longer one? Are we like clocks, at birth wound up at different tensions, to pass through the twenty-four hours at faster or slower rates, with each hour representing the crest of a different experience? Do the performance curves of different individuals likewise follow similar patterns of rising and falling, regardless of life span, or is a particular mental or emotional development of the shorter-lived one cut off by death?

With this question the biologist Raymond Pearl was much occupied. After a good deal of study he arrived at a kind of formula, namely that the duration of life in general varies inversely as the rate of life. The faster you live, the more you consume, and the shorter your existence. If the heart works faster, it won't work as long. Some persons have lived a whole lifetime by forty-five. However, the more you spread out your experiences, the longer you live. He therefore preached moderation.

The immediate problem of this paper is to consider the rate at which our mental abilities wax and wane and to determine to what extent we can retard these declines or at least salvage as much we can during the descending period. Arresting or cushioning decline is another way of prolonging life.

Psychological activities are dependent on physiological ones. The prevailing view is that physiological peaks are reached earlier than psychological ones.* Hence the more a mental activity in-

* There is a minority opinion, of which David Wechsler is a representative, which holds "that intellectual capacity begins to decline earlier rather than later

cludes a physiological factor, the more likely is it to undergo decline with age. The less any mental activity calls on physiological functions, the more it is likely to attain its maximum at a later age.

Because of this dependence of the mental on the physical, it will be helpful to consider for a moment the matter of physiological development.

According to Charlotte Buhler, from birth to fifteen growth is rapid. Around twenty-five the human physique is at its very best in strength and skill (muscular and physiological efficiency). We begin slowly descending from this level until forty-five, when the momentum increases; around fifty-five the rate again increases until seventy. Dr. Buhler finds that most Olympic champions and contestants fall in the age range twenty to twenty-eight. The peak of curves for ability in tennis, boxing, billiards, rifle and pistol shooting, and in big league baseball players is between twenty-five and thirty. The ability to undergo severe physical strain declines rapidly beyond thirty. In those sports, however, where a high degree of skill and fine adjustment are required but where there is a relatively little physical punishment, championships are won by men well up in the years.

Not all of the physical inadequacies of older people are due to the inescapable infirmities of age. Much of it results from neglect of physical condition and failure to keep up exercise. Lord Balfour played golf and tennis in his seventies. There are middle-aged champions in golf and polo. And in trapshooting some of the nationally known champions are men considerably beyond middle life. The war is also furnishing us with examples of men in military, industrial, and civilian life who, with training and under conditions of emergency, are able to rise to a level of performance deemed impossible in peacetime.

Again, while it is true that the physical infirmities of older men

---

than most physical capacities." However, there is no irreconcilable difference between this viewpoint and the more common one. Since particular physiological functions age at different rates, those which decline early will take with them the psychological activities dependent on them, even though intelligence considered in "global" fashion precedes in decline physiological functions also considered in total fashion.

constitute the greatest handicap in obtaining reëmployment, not all of these have been caused by age. Many of them are due to accidents which occurred in youth and early maturity. More than 2,400,000 industrial accidents occur yearly in the United States, of this number, one-half million take place in New York state alone. Of those rejected for reëmployment a large percentage, perhaps 50 percent, could be made physically fit for industrial work by medical treatment, since eyes, teeth, and hernia comprise 64 percent of all disabilities found.

Intelligence, considered as the effective organization of our mental abilities, at least as measureable by intelligence tests, matures very quickly, say between thirteen and sixteen, and stays on a level until the early twenties. Then this gain in ability of the last three years of mental age growth (thirteen to sixteen) is gradually lost in the next sixty years, with the larger portion of the decrements coming in the forties and sixties. By the age of fifty-five we have receded to the fourteen-year-old level. We gain mental stature quickly and lose it slowly.

However, if we consider separately the different abilities involved in that total functioning called "intelligence," we find that they do not all decline at the same rate.

In what follows, the abilities will be spread out in a kind of spectrum, starting with these mental abilities most dependent on physiological function, and ending up with those least so.

VISION AND HEARING

These functions, nonmental but a necessary foundation for those mental ones which are noted later, reach their peak in our late teens and then decline slowly in efficiency. One of the things which common knowledge most frequently associates with age is impaired eyesight and hearing.

A complicating factor in this matter of sensory deficiency is that with age there is a change, not only in perception but in emotional receptivity. Particularly in childhood and old age do we see and hear what we want to see and hear. As long as we live, each one of us is mainly concerned with the little world which he carries around inside of his skull. When old people find the world difficult and painful, not interested in them nor they in it, they may be tempted to shut it out by not hearing or seeing it.

Every handicap has two aspects. One is the handicap itself. The other is the way the handicap is used. Does the individual exploit deafness or poor vision, use these as excuses to relieve him from tasks and responsibilities? Or does he try to compensate for his handicaps as far as is humanly possible? This double aspect is true not only of declining sensory equipment but of all aging abilities, physical and mental.

REACTION TIME

Under this term we include alertness of attention and celerity of response. It is thus a combination of speed of perception, involving the senses of sight and hearing, and rapidity of muscular function (motor coördination). This ability reaches its peak in our late teens or early twenties. Of all the mental abilities it is the most dependent on physiological function and therefore shows the most marked loss. Exceptions exist, however, for in a particular experiment 25 percent of the seventy year olds had a reaction time equal to the average of the group, the latter covering the entire age range.

Life gives tests of reaction time when psychologists do not. Nation-wide surveys show that in automobile accidents involving pedestrians, two thirds of those killed are over forty. This is explained on the ground of impaired eyesight and hearing and general muscular slowing-up due to age. The next largest group of pedestrians killed consists of very young children. Someone said that he could raise the life expectancy a good many years if he only could achieve one result—keeping older people off the streets.

IMMEDIATE MEMORY

Although immediate memory reaches its peak in the late teens and early twenties, it declines rapidly with age. Our inability to remember recent events always has been recognized as a tell-tale sign of senescence. The old man can relate all that happened to him when he was a child, but where he placed a package earlier the same day completely escapes him. Observation and recall of what one has observed, such as events witnessed in motion pictures, also exhibits a gradual decline with age. According to H. L. Hollingworth, "The more recent impressions and experiences are the first to be lost; later those of adult life, then those of youth, and finally those of early childhood." Physiological changes are largely responsible for the inability to make fresh associations. The brain is no longer the soft phonograph disc of childhood; the brittle wax takes new impressions with difficulty, but the old ones are still deeply grooved there for the needle to follow. Old people talk more about the past because it has been better recorded, also because one's younger days are more emotionally toned, more tied up with a period of life in which hopes and desire for achievement and activity were at a maximum, and were either gratified or frustrated. Also, youth is a time when most persons have more emotional security and warm parental love than ever after.

It is interesting to note David Wechsler's remark that though memory declines with age it holds up better than certain other abilities, and that therefore "older people have other failings of which they might more reasonably complain than their poor memory."

NEW LEARNING

The work of Thorndike, Miles, and others offers experimental evidence that the ability to learn new things reaches its maximum in the late teens and early twenties and then starts slowly declining. In Thorndike's 1928 study there was a one percent loss in learning ability per year from age twenty-five on.

Jeanne G. Gilbert in her book *Mental Efficiency in Senescence* also reports that the type of learning in which loss is greatest is that of "paired associates." This is a relatively novel type of learning, requiring the formation of entirely new associations in which previously formed and accustomed habits of thought might interfere. The more a given task differs from an already existing habit pattern, the greater the loss in ability with age. However, immediate reproductive ability, such as making simple repetitions, shows relatively slight loss, which is also true of such examples of the older type of learning as general information and the giving of opposites.

As a correlate of this decline of learning ability, little change of interests is found after fifty. Most people tend to develop a pronounced dislike of any change as they approach old age. One's interests reflect the decrease in physical function, just as skills and abilities do. Strong found that with the years there is a lessening of interest in activities of a strenuous physical or mental sort: exploring, aviation, automobile driving; but there is an increase of interest in sedentary pursuits: enjoying one's home, visiting art galleries, reading detective stories, contributing to charities. There is a decrease in desire for occupational variety and in languages as such, though the interest in reading increases with age. Liking for amusements declines except for those of a distinctly cultural nature. Older men prefer, more than do younger men, amusements pursued alone. Fifty percent of this change of interest takes place between twenty-five and thirty-five; 20 percent between thirty-five and forty-five; 30 percent between forty-five and fifty-five. From fifty-five to sixty-five there is little or no change.

While there is a decrease in the amount of learning which persons acquire as they grow older, there are exceptional minds which possess the ability to continually renew themselves, to exploit to the fullest their intellectual resources. Even ordinary persons have far more ability and learning capacity than they ever utilize.

A good deal of the decreased physiological receptivity to new learning can be compensated for if the individual is interested in the present, and faces it bravely and zestfully. We have noted that the older person may use sensory loss as a way of defending himself and punishing a world he believes does not like or understand him, a state of mind often caused by the fact that he has allowed it to grow unfamiliar. And so he sheds all current experience as fast as it occurs.

If we reject people vocationally at forty or fifty, and give them no opportunity or reason for learning, we cannot be surprised by the results at sixty. Besides often lacking a financial or prestige incentive for acquiring new learning, they often lack the spontaneous interest. The men who at sixty-five or seventy voluntarily undertake a new job or profession or return to college; the ones who go in for amateur gardening, carpentry, or collecting—such men, because they are given a real incentive to show what they can do, often surprise themselves and us by the results. The older men and women who have been given a chance to work in war industries or engage in civilian defense activities have demonstrated an ability and usefulness that never would have been realized, either by them or by the community, except for the war. Some day every community will have its schools for older people with courses of study designed for the special needs, interests, and abilities of men and women in the sixties, seventies, and even eighties. Such schools will serve as demonstration centers of the possibilities for older people to acquire new learning. For whether it be in a school for the aged, in the office of the rehabilitator, in the factory, or in the occupational therapy department of a hospital, those older people who can still learn need to have this proved to them by the results of objective tests.

Part of the ostensible mental loss of older persons is simply the cumulative effect of poor work habits. The nature of the job or the life situation may encourage routine activities. Even assuming that men and women have started with a modest education and a knowledge of how to study, we cannot take them away from learning situations for decades and expect them to be receptive to new ideas. Most of us after sixty-five require a regimen of mental stimulation, or, as Dr. Lillien J. Martin puts it, we need an operation for the removal of "mental adhesions."

If activity is essential to the preservation of mental ability, this, incidentally, is one more reason why retirement is so unadvisable for many types of person, and why every union, every professional organization, even of those interested in the care of the aged, should have a department which will plan for retirement *to*, not retirement *from*, if retire we must. The industry or profession should retire people not on a particular day but over a period of years by means of a stepping-down and retraining process and through the medium of a Job Reallocation Bureau, operating within the industry or profession itself.

From the point of view of the best interests of most older persons, a regular job is necessary and desirable, assuming they are interested in working and physically and temperamentally able to cope with some type of regular employment.

OLD LEARNING

The ability to retain old learning shows much less decline with age than the capacity for acquiring new learning. Vocabulary may be taken as a chief example of old learning. But concerning the fate of vocabulary with age there is a good deal of controversy. Some students assert that it remains stationary; others, slightly in the majority, claim that it improves until the seventh or eighth decade and then begins to deteriorate.

In *Adult Intelligence* by Weisenberg, Roe, and McBride, the investigators found that the abilities sampled by non-language tests show an early peak, with a significant decline for the interval between age groups twenty through fifty-nine, reflecting declines in simpler motor and perceptual abilities, particularly those in which speed was a dominant factor. However, the authors found that the abilities sampled by most of the so-called language tests are well maintained through the thirties and in the majority of cases show only slight declines thereafter. The vocabulary tests proper show little or no decline through the fifties.

Vocabulary holds its own over the life span, first, because as earliest formed material it is not much affected by physiological decline. Second, it is learning that is constantly exercised. In fact, the world (that is, those who are not themselves aged) likes to believe that old people talk more than the young, or that a particular individual talks more in old age than he did in youth. But of this we have no objective evidence. What Peter has to say of Paul describes Peter as much as it does Paul. The so-called garrulity of the aged may really represent the non-aged's lack of interest in what they are saying. It is to young people that we would rather listen.

JUDGMENT AND REASONING ABILITY

This develops slowly in general or in a given field of work and reaches its peak latest of all abilities. It also is among the last to go. According to Walter R. R. Miles: * "In the test results for performance not necessitating quickness in reaction, but depending essentially on comprehension, reasoning and judgment; in matters where experience may contribute to the goodness of response; older adults appear most nearly to maintain their characteristic mature scoring level as long as they continue to maintain mental practice and intellectual interest."

The strategy of tackling problems often improves with age. Whenever knowledge of tactics, of varied ways of doing things is important, then it is that the older person is valued. The older doctor or lawyer, the craftsman, the political leader, the artist in living—all these can more than hold their own in competition with young people.

In tests of automobile driving it has been found that alertness in steering, quickness in braking, and speed of recovery from glare in night driving all decline with age and cause a large number of rejections on road tests. Harry Da Silva, a leading authority, observes,† "Although this decline of ability is important and should be recognized and allowed for by persons as they grow older, it has too often been exaggerated. The assets of the older persons, such as improved judgment, better emotional control and coolness in the face of emergencies, usually more than offset the slight loss of sensory capacity and motor control. Older drivers prefer to drive more slowly and are apparently more careful. In tests of adaptability and vigilance, older experienced drivers invariably rank higher than young ones."

Statistics show that it is the young age groups that are mostly involved in driving accidents. The average motorist of fifty drives about four times as far without accident as the average driver of

* "Psychological Aspects of Ageing," in *Problems of Ageing*, edited by E. V. Cowdry (Baltimore, Williams & Wilkins, 1942), p. 771.

† "Age and Highway Accidents," *Scientific Monthly*, XLVII (Dec., 1938), 536–45.

twenty. But neither the youthful driver in his teens and twenties nor the elderly driver in the fifties or sixties is as safe as the adult between forty-five and fifty-two. There are fewer drivers on the road beyond fifty, and although they drive less distance their accident rate starts to increase again.

With respect to industrial accidents, the complaint that the older worker has an undue number of accidents is without foundation. Figures prepared by the New York State Department of Labor for 1937 show that proneness to accidents is greatest in the age group twenty to twenty-four, least in the older group. A group of Boston bus drivers outstanding for safety of performance averaged fifty years of age. Age-accident statistics of a military accident insurance company as compiled by Marbe reveal that the group of men in the range twenty-seven to fifty-eight have 40 percent fewer accidents than those in the age range sixteen to twenty-one. These results, Marbe claims, are not due to the fact that older men have less hazardous tasks but rather to a certain characteristic foolhardiness and failure to recognize danger on the part of the younger groups. Carefulness, good judgment, and experience on the part of the older worker result in fewer accidents.

In a steel plant, workers with ten to fifteen years' experience had one fourteenth as many accidents as those with six months' experience. In a Connecticut silk mill, workers sixty years of age and over had only one fifth as many accidents as the workers under nineteen years of age. Though accident frequency diminishes with age, accident severity increases. If we are to take days absent as a check, with advancing age recuperation is probably slower, and older men may be less eager about returning to work. Concerning the older person's greater freedom from accidents, it is worth noting Pressey's observation that in any particular organization there is a progressive selection of the better workers and a weeding out of the unfit.

In the years to come, we shall have to develop a whole repertory of ways to utilize the judgment and experience of older people, whether these be in an advisory and teaching capacity, in the field of family and home relations, in industry, or in some directing work of an educational, social service, or recreational character.

Advisory functions might best be exercised within the family but as we see elsewhere in this volume, particularly in Miss Randall's paper, the generations are not always amicably disposed toward each other. Hence, a clearinghouse by means of which an older individual might find young people to guide would help keep his interest alive and his mind active. Many young people who have no families to help them decide and solve important problems in life might be glad to adopt godparents, and the latter would be glad to give of their judgment and experience. Interesting possibilities lie in setting up correspondence friendships between old and young. I have heard of an ex-schoolteacher in a New York City old age home who assists some Southern children with their lessons and who also helps prepare lesson material for their teacher. There is a great waste in not using the wisdom of older people, concerning which John Dewey writes: "I am unable to see how the basic human problem can be solved without social changes which ensure first to every individual the chance to have intrinsically worth-while experience as long as he lives and second to provide significant socially useful outlets for the maturity and wisdom gained by experience." *

CREATIVE IMAGINATION

This apparently is ageless. To test the imagination, Miles used the Kinephantom—a revolving fan whose silhouette appears like an animated ink blot. Subjects were required to interpret these silhouettes. Miles found that younger and older individuals in an average population achieved practically the same scores.

The creative impulse has been intensively studied by Harvey C. Lehman, and reported upon in a series of papers mostly published in *Scientific Monthly*. Lehman is interested, not in the creativity of the ordinary person, but in the genius, the extraordinary performer—intellectually and artistically. Such a performer cannot be adequately evaluated by any single psychologist or other individual but only by a consensus of experts in the specialized field.

Lehman finds that the chronological age at which one is most

* Introduction to *Problems of Ageing*, edited by E. V. Cowdry, 2d edition, p. xxxii.

likely to do his most important work varies with the nature of the task. For many activities there exists a relatively brief interval during which groups of individuals will be most likely to attain their greatest success. For several kinds of creative thinking, the peaks are at ages 35–39. This is true in philosophy and in medicine. In music certain types of composers reach their height in the same age range, 35–39; other types reach theirs between 40 and 44. Authors of best books and military leaders also reach their peaks between 40 and 44. But with respect to the political ladder, the top is most likely to be reached by men who are between 50 and 59. While Lehman would place the peak of human physical strength and skill at about 27 or 28, he finds that not until approximately thirty years later does man attain full political stature.

In some respects young and old are in a state of constant competition. But if there is one area in which the older age groups have been most successful it is in the struggle for leadership as exemplified in the business and political fields.

When our work depends largely on physiological activity, greater achievements like lesser ones in the same fields will come earlier; when it depends on psychological factors to a relatively greater extent, the unique system or formulation tends like other products of mature experience and generalized judgment to appear later. Dorland offers data drawn from 400 eminent persons which are illuminating in this respect. The average age at which their masterpieces were produced runs as follows: physicists, 41; inventors, poets, dramatists, and playwrights, 44; novelists, 46; explorers and warriors, 47; actors and musical composers, 48; artists and divines, 50; reformers and essayists, 51; physicians, surgeons, and statesmen, 52; philosophers, 54; astronomers and mathematicians, satirists, and humorists, 56; historians, 57; jurists and naturalists, 58.

Fulton found the age of authorship of 76 most important works in the history of physiology to be: men under forty, 45 percent; men over forty, 55 percent.

It is Lehman's general conclusion that individuals may think creatively and make invaluable contributions at practically every chronological age level beyond early youth. It is merely a question of when a gifted person produces either his masterpiece or the greatest quantity of high-quality performances. Thorndike in 1928 showed that with respect to the age at master work: 22 of a group of 91 scientists and 19 out of a sample of 80 men of affairs produced their greatest achievement after the age of sixty, and in the case of six of the scientists, their chief contribution came after the age of eighty.

Lehman quotes with approval a statement on this subject by Robert Sessions Woodworth, which appeared originally in a letter privately communicated to Dr. Lehman. Writes Woodworth: *

> Another condition favorable to invention is youth, or at least comparative youth, with its openness to new impressions and its radical tendency to do something different from what has been done before. Maturity also is necessary for socially important creative work. Boys and girls seldom write, or paint, discover or invent anything of social value, not having as yet acquired the necessary groundwork of their art or science. But in the twenties or thirties, originality should show itself. Often a great producer goes on improving his style till well along in life, but most of the real novelties come from the years 25–45. It would be foolish to draw a dead line anywhere. Goethe at 80 finally writing down a scene of Faust, Second Part, which he had conceived at 30, and feeling that the delay had been desirable for the increased knowledge it had given of the world—Darwin, giving out his theory of evolution at 50 after over twenty years of collecting data to test the hypothesis which he had conceived at 28—Handel, working into his masterpiece, *The Messiah*, at the age of 56 the airs originally composed for his early operas—are instances of the effective combination of youthful inventiveness with mature sureness of judgment, in the production of great works of invention.

Before we can arrive at any final conclusion concerning the reduction in achievement with age, we should ponder on the following questions which Lehman raises:

> Can intelligence be disentangled from such other factors as motivation to learn, pressure to utilize fully what has been learned, the plasticity of the nervous system, relatively fixed; unalterable habits, level of functioning, physical stamina, environmental opportunity? Is it possible

* In H. C. Lehman and W. S. Gamertsfelder, "Man's Creative Years in Philosophy," *Psychological Review*, XLIX (July, 1942), 341–42.

to motivate the older individual to the same extent that the youth can be motivated, if the oldster has attained many of his life goals and if the youth has reached few of his goals? Is it valid to assume that in our rapidly changing civilization the older adult has had the same intellectual diet and opportunity to learn, as has the younger adult? *

In addition to the elements Lehman mentions as influencing intellectual functioning, there is one—a good emotional adjustment—which is essential to continued utilization of whatever mental efficiency one possesses. Many emotional factors which are unrelated to age or to intellectual decline as such may lead to a spurious deterioration. Among these are the following: family dissensions; feeling of inadequacy; pressure, real or imaginary, from a superior or from youthful competition; money difficulties; an insecure job; the first birthday of one of the later decades; unemployment. It is fear of aging, rather than the aging process itself, which often causes a functional loss in the mental realm, just as it does in the physical. Anticipating the loss of efficiency, we hasten the arrival of what we expect. If the confidence in one's ability is essential at earlier life periods, it is most important during senescence.

Physical well-being is bound up with the preservation of mental efficiency. Only recently have we begun to realize the importance in this connection of diet, for example. In September, 1942, a symposium "Vitamins and Nutrition" was held under the auspices of the American Chemical Society. At this symposium, Drs. McCay, James, and Barnes of Cornell University described some experiments on puppies which led them to believe that the normal span of life could be stretched out considerably by the ingestion of a diet low in calories and high in the quality of its nutritional elements—proteins, minerals, and vitamins. In particular, the experimenters felt that such a diet would preserve intellectual capacity over a much longer period.

This brief review of the way our mental abilities wax and wane leads to certain conclusions. Few people live long enough to undergo severe obsolescence of *all* abilities and functions. General

* H. C. Lehman, "The Creative Years: Medicine, Surgery, and Certain Related Fields," *Scientific Monthly*, LII (May, 1941), 461.

decline or deterioration (complete senility) is rare. We therefore should speak not of an aged person, but an aged ability, function, or adjustment, whether it be physical, mental, emotional, social, vocational, or a subdivision of any one of these areas.

Not so long ago the insane individual was put away in a cell and regarded as incurable. Only yesterday old people were similarly thought of as a total loss. However, we are today witnessing the advent of a new attitude, namely, that often much can be salvaged from later maturity. Instead of pitting age against youth, we should strive to realize the potentialities of each. Coöperation, rather than competition, will bring out the best in each age grouping. The first one to publicize the point of view that by using the proper measuring and rehabilitating instruments we can compensate for the decline of age and outwit its handicaps was Dr. Lillien J. Martin, who at the age of seventy started the San Francisco Old Age Center in 1921. Until her death in March, 1943, at the age of ninety-two, she was active in her consulting work with aged clients.

By means of tests of psychological abilities, it is possible to determine the extent of mental deterioration and the degree to which particular losses are permanent. If, after an evaluation of life history and an appraisal of the present daily program and interests, rehabilitation is decided upon, the individual is put through a program of remedial exercises which in some persons may serve to retard the process of mental deterioration and even to reverse it.*

Particularly important in the rehabilitation of an older person is the life history. All of us pursue several lives which run parallel on different levels. First, there is the one we think we are leading, one mostly made up of longing, aspiration, day-dreaming. Second, there is the life that others think we are having. Then, there is the life we actually have led. A great need of older people is that of reinterpreting their experiences, fusing together their several lives into one self, with which they can dwell peacefully the rest of their days. The writer has found the life history, as utilized in the form of his questionnaire for the study of later adjustments, quite

* A detailed discussion of this topic will be found in the writer's "Psychological Guidance for Older Persons," in Cowdry, *Problems of Ageing*, 2d ed., revised.

effective in achieving this educational and semi-therapeutic effect.

Sidney Pressey* points out that world records in most sports continue to be broken. Some of this improvement he believes is due to better techniques in the sport and better methods of training. A number of notable athletes, moreover, have had to overcome serious physical handicaps in order to achieve championship distinction—Glenn Cunningham, for example. If effort and practice expertly directed may bring about marked gains, there are unsuspected potentialities in almost everyone. True, it is, that we age physically and that mental functions dependent on physiological efficiency must also age. The important fact, however, is whether the old person attempts to overcome or ignore the effect of these changes or whether he lets himself be overwhelmed by them. His attitude and the world's attitude toward the declines act and react on each other. If he tends to disregard the changes the world will also, and vice versa. An older person determined to utilize his resources to the maximum might raise his general level of fitness to a degree now thought impossible of realization.

However, we mustn't deceive ourselves. There is decline with the years. As long as we include speed factors in our appraisal technique we will find a difference in efficiency between a group of persons in the sixties and one in the twenties. By the age of seventy, there will be an average decrement in strength, skill, and sensory acuity of one fourth to one third from the twenty-five year old average. Dr. Jeanne G. Gilbert in her study *Mental Efficiency in Senescence* found an efficiency index of 4.8 years difference between the sixties and twenties. In the sixties themselves the 65–69 individuals were found by Gilbert to be inferior in mental efficiency to those 60–64.

If we eliminate speed and consider only mental power, the difference between older and younger individuals is reduced. Intellectual persistence, a non-speed factor, does not show age decrement. Even with regard to mental efficiency, individual differences may be as great at the older ages as at the younger, and about 25 percent

* S. L. Pressey, Raymond G. Kuhlen, J. E. Janney, *Life: a Psychological Survey* (New York, Harper and Brothers, 1939).

of the oldest men appear to do as well as the average young adults in tests of strength, skill, and sensory acuity. However, not all high scores were achieved by the young, nor low ones by old. In most types of work, the decrease should not be important and might well be more than balanced by greater experience and dependability. As Pressey * says: "To the average person, it is of little practical importance that he cannot run as fast at sixty as he can at thirty; at all ages, the usual pace in self-locomotion is the walk."

In the literature, particularly in the writings of Lorge and of Gilbert, we find the opinion that the higher the original intellectual endowment, the slighter the decline—barring disease, injury, or other untoward circumstances. The more unusually gifted we are in a particular ability, the longer and the more of that ability we are likely to retain. The lower the initial equipment, the more rapid the decline. A superior individual will even in old age exceed the average of the young.

It may be true that there are only a small number of individuals in the sixties capable of attacking with normal efficiency (that is, as speedily) tasks involving *new* learning suited to their native intellect. It is not true, however, that age alone is a sufficient factor by which to judge one's efficiency in his own particular work, since judgment, better integration of knowledge, and practice over a long period of years compensates for losses in motor dexterity and sensory acuity. The older individual retains almost unimpaired his capacity for solving mental problems of equal difficulty to those he could solve when younger. Older men generally are not suitable for active duty as policemen or firemen, or in other pursuits that require long periods of sustained physical activity, exposure to danger of bodily harm, dexterity of the hands, agility of the limbs. But when a more thoughtful application to the work at hand is needed, there is no reason to say older workers cannot serve as well or better than younger ones.

Miles finds that on the basis of his chronological age alone, "it is scarcely possible to predict an individual's intelligence score to a degree much better than chance. The persistence from decade to

* Pressey, Kuhlen, and Janney, *Life: a Psychological Survey*, p. 153.

decade of score differences in terms of occupation or education points to a contrast among individuals, and in groups, of greater importance industrially and socially than the demonstrated age differences*. . . . Experience and experiment show that perception is not as prompt in the old as in the young and that its span is shorter. But neither speed of activity nor speed of perception are adequate criteria for work and worker value. Persistence in effort and in practice with materials used compensates to some extent in producing a more even work rate and product. Interest and skill are basic in such compensation and they tend in paths other than the simple automatic ones to counterbalance the decline in perceptive ability with its correlate of decrease in work rate†. . . . Formulations regarding his life goals and evaluations of the extent to which an individual has organized his energy for reaching these objectives would probably serve us at present as better bases for intelligence tests, score prediction and intellectual classification than the more definitely measurable datum of age." ‡

This statement emphasizes once again that the indiscriminate and arbitrary shelving of men and women merely for age inflicts a great loss upon society and individual. If we shift workers over from those jobs involving speed and strength, to those utilizing skills which age does not impair, we can prolong the working lives of many older men and women.

In the next decade or two the study of mental abilities in the aged will be almost as common as that of children today, and vocational guidance based on a knowledge of when old people are weak and when strong will be possible. If at sixty-five many of the persons retired could still continue working at their jobs with earlier efficiency, or do well at simpler jobs, what shall we say of age forty as a deadline? It was utter nonsense in pre-war days (and it will be again in post-war days) to say that men and women over forty have undergone so marked a decline in essential mental abilities that as a group they are no longer employable in most trades. In a thirty

* "Psychological Aspects of Ageing," in E. V. Cowdry, *Problems of Ageing*, 2d ed., 1942, p. 770. The material quoted has been somewhat rearranged by the Editor.

† *Ibid.*, p. 764.

‡ *Ibid.*, p. 770.

year old, inefficiency is merely inefficiency. In a sixty year old, it is senility. A young fool is a fool. But when he has lived a long time, he is no longer a fool. He is old.

One question which every person who deals with older people must ask himself, whether he be a social worker, superintendent of old age homes, or physician, is this, "Are the experiences which I provide or advise for my client calculated to provide mental stimulation, enlarge his horizons and thus aid in preserving his intellectual abilities?" We can answer this only by dealing with a preliminary question, namely; "In the typical institution for older people, or in the service available to recipients of old age assistance or social security, how much do we find of challenge, problem solving, the novel and the unpredictable?" It may be that most old people cannot assimilate much new experience. But before we accept that as a universal and immutable psychological law we must discover how much new experience our culture makes available for them.

Providing the older person with suitable occupational and recreational outlets is not an easy matter. The individual with trained intelligence and education is better able to adapt himself to sedentary and to socially isolated activities than is the former manual worker. For example, what can we do in an old age home where all the residents were once domestics? The immediate solution would be real jobs of a simplified and part-time nature, aided and abetted by occupational therapy and the usual recreational devices appealing to persons of limited educational experience. The best solution is a long term one, namely, to have continuous additional education at pre-senescent age levels. Every large factory, business organization, and union should have educational and recreational programs for each worker, adjusting this to his changing needs as the worker grows older. A program providing for one's time during the post-employment period should be drawn up by management and worker while the latter is still employed.

A woman of seventy-six came to an old age home unable to play the piano. After two years of assiduous practice, she is considered an able performer, at least by her fellow members. Dr. Lillien J. Martin learned to drive a car at seventy-seven. However, many older persons, if they cannot continue with their old interests, will have nothing at all, since they either refuse or are unable to take on new hobbies and interests. Other old people also want mainly to rest. Having done tedious or back-breaking labor all their lives, they naturally are unenthusiastic about the notion of a "continuous work-like program as long as life lasts."

Those dealing with the aged are often faced with a decision to let a person "rest," if that is what he wants. However, an older person often thinks he is through and acts on this conviction though he may still be capable of much activity and experiencing. The emotionally normal individual wants to continue a life filled with at least a moderate amount of feeling and action. He who, not physically incapacitated, wants to spend all his time "resting," in reality is running away from life. This he does either because of past failures, fear of future ones, or because he feels his efforts will be inadequately rewarded.

Every organization devoted to the care and happiness of older people should have on its staff one person of imagination, initiative and patience who will act as a link with activities in the outside world. Such a liaison officer will arrange for talks on current events, and for theater and motion picture parties (often without charge, if slack times are selected). It will be he who makes arrangements for spiritual adoption by the oldsters of younger people and families on the outside, and who looks for volunteer and part-time positions—all in order that old people may be kept in contact with the present and avoid the growth of the hard mental shell that isolates them from the world of living just as if it were a premature entombment.

It is interesting to speculate on whether those who work with older people age quicker than those who deal with younger groups. In general, the more mentally stimulating the employee's environment, the longer he will retain his intellectual abilities at their maximum, assuming he depends on his job for stimulation. If his task is humdrum and routine, he can either change his approach to his job so that he sees it in a new light or else obtain his stimulation outside of working hours. But if he doesn't get it either on the job or outside of it, he will age faster mentally than he would otherwise.

Retirement on pension, medical care, old age homes—none of these measures solves the problem of older people. Would financial support and medical care solve the problem of children and young people? No one denies that as we grow older there is a change in the type of experience possible or a lessening in the amount of achievement we can have even in those experiences that remain. Part of this may be due to the physical limitations of old age, but as much arises from a deficiency in the powers of imaginative projection and in a lack of ingenuity, both on the part of the aged and on the part of those who live with them in family groups or who are entrusted with the task of "servicing" them.

Life is always ending and always beginning. Never lacking is the challenge of discovering the particular fulfillments and achievements that are possible at each age, in each situation or under each handicap. Our existence is a journey. Let us hope that the traveler gets his quota of fresh and novel experiences en route. But if the experiences and views remain the same, he can bring to them at least a new attitude, a new method of observation.

Best for old people would be real jobs, real family relationships, real functioning in society. But if they cannot be given real lives, they must have proxy ones. Nine million old people today, twenty-six million in 1980, cannot be relegated to lives of suspended animation. The aged need schools, recreation centers, arts and crafts centers, sheltered work shops, adult playgrounds, marriage brokers, social clubs. They need bureaus for the exchange of services. The retired carpenter, doctor, teacher, nurse, painter, gardener—all have something to contribute to each other and themselves. The Universal School of Handicrafts in New York City which has had unusual success with older people, finds that "creative expression has great therapeutic power and may prevent mental and physical deterioration." Since the human imagination knows no age barrier, men and women as long as they live can make things of beauty with their own hands. Certainly in any program of aiding the aged, occupational therapy holds tremendous possibilities. However they be achieved, recreational and creative activity, personal fulfillment and education, drawing from society and contributing to society, need never end.

In a letter which the writer received recently from an eminent American psychologist there were these lines: "More ought to be known about senescence. My own advancing age is really quite an interesting affair to me as I see the changes coming about." What more admirable attitude could there be than that of William McAdoo who said in his last years, "My life has covered a wide range and it has been full of interesting and unexpected adventure. I have no quarrel with Fate, no matter in what moods I have found her and no matter what her decrees have been. I have had a glorious time!" Then there are the extraordinary last words of the late Earl Balfour, who as his eyes closed in death whispered, "This is going to be a great experience." Any person who can continue to meet every changing vista or circumstance in terms of its power, not for hurt but for enlightenment or stimulation, need not fear mental decline, waning physical powers, loneliness, misfortune. He has learned the art of growing old successfully.

THE OLDER PERSON IN THE CHANGING SOCIAL SCENE

By Lawrence K. Frank *

THE WORDS "a changing society" are being constantly used but we are not always clear just what they mean. Usually we refer to the more or less outward, visible signs of new developments in our economic and industrial life and to some of the modifications in living which we have been forced to make to meet such developments. Urbanization, with the consequent crowding of more and more people into large cities, is perhaps one of the most striking of these changes and one that is responsible for much maladjustment and disturbance, since the older patterns of rural living which are carried into the city are either inefficient or in conflict with the other demands of city life. Within the city we have witnessed in recent years the rise of congregate dwellings or apartment houses in which a thousand or more persons may live, and very recently we have seen the construction of large-scale housing developments which provide housing for twenty to thirty thousand persons in what would be a large town or small city.

Another prominent, inescapable feature of social change is seen in the organization of rapid transportation and communication with automobiles and buses, streamlined trains and airplanes, which now enable us to move about from place to place and to communicate with almost unbelievable speed. Similarly we have seen the rise of large-scale commercial amusements in the form of moving pictures and radio, and the big sport events such as baseball and football, attended by many thousands of spectators. These amusements are notable because they are largely enjoyed by the individual who passively attends with little or no effort; indeed, they are sometimes

* Writer on sociological and psychological subjects, formerly Vice-President, Josiah Macy, Jr., Foundation.

likened to anodynes and drugs to which individuals turn for escape or forgetfulness.

These developments that have so immediately affected family and individual living are, however, but products of an even more amazing development of industries and public utilities that now furnish an unbelievable variety of goods and services as modern technology is increasingly focused upon production. From the factories have come forth a wide variety of equipment and gadgets and so-called labor-saving devices, together with machines and tools that have now supplanted most earlier handicrafts and operations. These developments have also had an immediate influence upon daily living to the extent that they have led to the establishment of central heating and hot-water supplies, canning factories, commercial bakeries, laundries, restaurants, and modern hospitals and schools that have progressively taken over the former functions and duties of the home.

These large-scale social, economic, and industrial changes have transformed our social life and have had an impact upon daily living that we are only just beginning to realize. To the older men and women, especially those who grew up in the simpler rural life of a generation or two ago, they present a bewildering array of new situations to which adjustments may be difficult. Even the acceptance and use of modern conveniences may, because of their complexity and speed, present very difficult situations, as we may see in the hestitation of older people to enter moving stairways and elevators and their avoidance of the labor-saving gadgets with which modern life is now equipped. It is to be noted that it is not only the complexity of these newer devices and equipment, but the speed with which they operate that often creates anxiety for the older person whose reactions are slower than those of the average person to whom, after all, the contrivance is geared.

In considering the impact of the changing social scene upon the older person today, we should recognize these difficulties and try to realize how trying, if not exhausting, the effort to keep on being alert must be to those who no longer can have the quickness of perception and response of the younger person.

It is customary, in discussing our changing socio-economic life to think of these developments as essentially novel and modern, but a little reflection will remind us that the process of socio-economic change has been under way for almost two hundred years in England and later in this country. Let us recall how England was disrupted about 1750 with the coming of machinery and urbanization; of how the older handicrafts were ruined as factories arose; and how the simpler agricultural life was supplanted as England became increasingly industrialized. These changes brought large-scale political upheavals and social strife which were more or less duplicated in this country following the Civil War. The novel *Inheritance* by Phyllis Bentley gives a poignant picture of how the decline and closing of handicrafts and the development of industrialization led to social changes which affected people of different social classes, economic classes, and age groups.

Within the past thirty or forty years, however, there has been an intensification of all these trends and it may be truly said that the social, economic, and technological changes have been coming more rapidly and on a larger scale than ever before. Indeed, it may be said that much of the present-day confusion and conflict arises from the long delayed and strongly resisted readjustments in our social and political life to meet these other developments, and that now we are faced with widespread disturbances and violence because we have not modified our laws and customs to bring them into greater conformity with our economic and industrial development.

Discussions of these larger impersonal developments in industry and technology often fail to give us a clear picture of what they mean to the individual man and woman. Let us try to see a little more clearly how these changes do affect our ways of life. Perhaps the most notable and often the most neglected aspect of recent social change is seen in the way in which we have given up *making* a living in order to *earn* a living; that is to say, more and more we are engaged in wage-earning, even in agriculture, where farming has been shifted to cash crops. This means that our economic security is no longer a question of how much effort we can put into work, but rather depends upon the shifting fortunes of business enterprise.

Along with this change from making to earning a living we should note the passing of the family homestead, so that now few of us have any permanent home or abode, but rather move about from dwelling to dwelling in accordance with the changing requirements of jobs and business conditions. As we have been engaged in trying to earn a more or less precarious living and have shifted our dwellings from place to place, we have had to face the further difficulty that, until the 1940 national defense program began, industry has insisted upon earlier retirement. Before the war it was not infrequent for wage earners to be retired at forty-five as no longer capable of meeting the demands of the rapid pace of industrial processes. This latter situation was indeed ironical, since during the last generation men and women have been living longer but found that they were no longer needed in business and economy. The war, of course, has changed this situation, though whether such change is temporary it is hard to say at present.

I was recently impressed with comments in Washington concerning what is happening in industries today. The larger, more far-sighted, better financed industries are beginning to make a conscious effort to provide opportunities for older and for handicapped workers. Six or seven years ago anyone with any kind of heart affliction would have been ruled out for employment. Industry now provides him with a job that he can safely do and gives him the medical supervision and direction that he needs to maintain himself under working conditions. This may mark a new trend in work for older individuals. In a Midwest factory there is one man, approximately eighty years of age, whom the company brings in a car every morning and returns home in similar fashion every evening. This old man does nothing except keep up the morale of the fifty, sixty, or seventy year old people who have the skill which that factory requires.

If we will reflect on what it means to have no permanent place of abode or roots in the community, to be largely at the mercy of fluctuating business conditions, to face early retirement—we will begin to get a clearer view of what changing socio-economic conditions are meaning to the individual man and woman as he or she grows older.

Here it is appropriate to point out that along with the developments in our social, economic, and industrial activities there has been a progressive shift in our population which has been scarcely realized except by special students of the subject. During the nineteenth century the population of the United States increased at a prodigious pace both through the high birth rate and through the entrance of numerous immigrants from abroad. Within the last thirty to forty years the birth rate has been almost steadily declining, and the duration of life has been extended. Whereas in 1900 our population could be represented by a pyramid with a broad base of children under five, tapering to an apex of a few older persons, today our population may be represented by a figure resembling a barrel, with a rapidly decreasing number of children at the bottom, and a growing number of individuals over seventy at the top, with a large bulge in the middle years of twenty to forty-five. According to the best estimates of our future population, in another forty years, if present trends continue, our population picture may be likened to that of a candle with an equal number of males and females in each age from one year up to approximately seventy, when there will be a slight taper where the wick would appear. The present and prospective population situation is indeed unique, since so far as we know it has never existed before, at least in western European culture. This very change in the age distribution of our population, with the declining number of babies and children and the increasing number of older men and women, presents a situation that calls for large-scale social, economic, and political readjustments for which we have scarcely begun to prepare.

It should be recalled that in earlier times only a few older persons survived the hazards and strains of life, and accordingly they enjoyed prestige and widespread respect and exercised the authority which their age and supposed wisdom deserved. Today and in the immediate future we face a situation in which there will be an increasing number of older men and women who, largely because of rapid social changes, are confused and bewildered and only too often resistant to the enforced readjustments, so that they enjoy little prestige and can exercise little or no authority, except in so far as they may, through the organization of political pressure groups, force from society various concessions like these being urged today by the organizations of older persons through the country.

The difficult readjustments we face in meeting the changing economic and industrial situations are no greater than those which confront us in the rapid increase in the number of older men and women in our population, for which we have at present made little or no systematic preparation. We should recognize that there is a certain irony in this situation, inasmuch as we face more rapid and more extensive changes calling for even greater social reorganization at a time when apparently our population will have an increasing number of older individuals who, in general, will be less capable of meeting such situations and of accepting the necessary social changes involved.

The enactment of old age security provisions within the last few years may be regarded as the first step toward meeting the requirements of our aging population. It is worth pointing out that for years business and industry have recognized the necessity of replacing machinery and equipment and have, in accordance with good accounting practice, set up reserves to meet the cost of such retirements. Only recently, however, have we recognized the necessity for meeting human obsolescence and depreciation by providing old age retirements as a justifiable charge upon industry. Perhaps we can interpret this as a sign of the progress of the democratic aspiration toward recognizing the integrity of the individual personality and attempting to protect and conserve individuals.

Both in childhood and in old age the necessity for large-scale social provisions is gradually being recognized though a variety of provisions designed to conserve our human resources in all possible ways. Such provisions as have now been made, however, are the first faltering steps toward a more systematic social program that will arise as we begin to assay all our social life and institutions, business, industry, professions, government, education, and so forth, in terms of what they are doing to and for the individual.

While we have been often told that social change is caused by inventions and discoveries which are bringing about alterations in our economic life, it is also worth noting that many social changes are the result of a change in sensibilities, that is, through new awareness of human needs and values which were formerly ignored or sacrificed, sudden realization of injustices we can no longer tolerate as humanly desirable. Thus, as we could complacently accept the exploitation of individuals, we could tolerate the almost unbelievable cruelty and destruction of men and women and children that was so frequent during the nineteenth century both here and abroad. Today, as we become increasingly sensitive to human needs and begin to place a value upon the individual, we are more and more ready to realize how ruthlessly destructive our social life has been. Emphasizing the importance of sensibilities and values, therefore, is justified here because it is just this sensitive awareness which our teachers and educators must create and communicate to others if we are to hope for any approach to a more humanly decent society. The fundamental conflict is between technology and human sensibilities, between forms of production and our consciousness. The rise of new sensibilities, becoming aware of human values and needs, may represent a change which in the long run will be more important than technology because these sensibilities will dictate to what use to put our science and technology.

Let us remind ourselves that the basic social question with which economics, political science, and sociology are concerned may be formulated in terms of "who shall be sacrificed for whom?" How sensitive are we to the rights of people who are being sacrificed? In the past the ruthless using or exploitation of individuals has been justified by all manner of social theories and by our basic cultural traditions. Here we should pause to discuss what our culture is and does, since these cultural changes have large significance for the life of the older individual. The better understanding we can gain of what our culture means, both to the group and to the individual, the better position we shall be in to understand some of the most acute difficulties that are faced by older individuals in their personal lives today.

Perhaps we can gain a better understanding of what we mean by culture by realizing that as organisms we exist in the geographical environment or space that we call nature, but that as members of society we carry on our life activities in what might be called social space, utilizing the institutions of contract, barter, sale, courtship, marriage, divorce, property owning, and litigation to regulate our activities and our conduct toward others.

Until recently we have been inclined to think of our social life and of our culture as some sort of large-scale organization or mechanisms existing somewhere between the earth and sky and operating by some cosmic forces, for example, economic forces, social forces, and so forth. Today we are beginning to realize that what we call organized society is not a cosmic organization, but rather is to be looked upon as the patterned conduct of individuals who have been taught in childhood what to do and not to do, what to say, what to believe, and what to think, so that in a very real sense society and culture are really built into us in the basic ideas and beliefs and assumptions, the selective awareness, patterns of conduct, cherished goals and aspirations to which we devote our lives, and in the criteria of credibility, that is, the way we judge what we will believe or disbelieve.

Each individual child must be inducted into a particular social life and a particular culture and be made to see, believe, and feel in accordance with our social and cultural traditions. Likewise each individual child undergoes the process of molding his naïve impulsive behavior into the patterned conduct, especially as seen in his habits of eating and elimination, his emotional reactions, and all the other patterns of socialized behavior which enable him to participate in the group life.

Now the most interesting and significant aspect of this whole process is that each individual child, while learning to conform more or less to the standardized requirements of our society, nevertheless builds up a highly individualized version of the required conduct and, above all, his own peculiar way of feeling toward situations and people. It is not unwarranted, therefore, to say that while we exist in the geographical environment of nature and carry on our life activities in the social world, business, industry, government, the family, we really live in the *private world* of our own personality.

Let me illustrate this by pointing out that when we listen to someone speaking, each of us sees a different person, hears different remarks, and reacts to what we hear with approval or dislike, so that when we come from any meeting with others we remember and quote not what was said, but rather what we heard. We should realize, therefore, that each one of us is living in this highly idiomatic private world that we have developed from our life experience and that to a larger extent than we may care to recognize, our whole adult life is governed by our forgotten childhood, when we were being socialized and made a participating member of our social and cultural life. During those early but forgotten years we developed our basic patterns of conduct, our characteristic ways of accepting and organizing experience and our persistent ways of feeling toward the world, especially the feelings of anxiety, guilt, and resentment or hostility. These feelings color the world in every situation in which we find ourselves, and because they derive from those early years for which we have no conscious memory, we rarely, if ever, have any insight into our own conduct or that of others. Social change is not something that is going on outside, however much it may appear in changed equipment. Social change, if there is any, is the change taking place in human behavior, and society and culture is an aggregate consisting of the ways you and I believe, feel, and act about our lives and the lives of other individuals. It is the common elements of speech and patterns of conduct that make up the thing called society, and that is changing because you and I have ceased to obey implicitly the ideas and patterns of conduct taught to us by our teachers, parents, and others in our youth. Irrespective of whether social conditions change as we grow older—the exceptions to which are the accustomed patterns of action—people are changing.

If we will now apply this discussion to the situation of the older person we may gain some light on what the changing social scene means to an aging individual. The private world which he built many years ago may become increasingly incompatible with the changing social situation. The basic assumptions and beliefs with which the individual in early life attempted to make life meaningful and to organize his experience become increasingly obsolete and incredible in the life of today. The patterns of conduct which the individual learned in early life with the sanction of law, the church, and the community mores, become increasingly inadequate as the various social changes we have discussed before crowd in upon him and demand readjustments that are more and more difficult to make. Thus, for the older person we may say that it becomes increasingly difficult to bring life experience within the range of the patterns of personal thinking, acting, and feeling that constitute his only repertory for living. As old friends and family disappear his feeling of isolation grows, and he finds situations more and more perplexing and refractory. The older patterns with which he met life in his childhood and youth, however inadequate and difficult then, are now becoming almost impossible for utilization in the new situations and with the younger people who have grown up with other ideas and beliefs and ways of living.

We should pause here to point out that the whole emphasis of education in the home and family, in the church and school, has been to establish more or less rigid patterns of thinking and acting, and to demand a high degree of conformity which may operate to unfit the individual to meet changes in his later life. It is not unwarranted to say that, perhaps unconsciously but more or less effectively, the educational process through which the individual passes seems almost deliberately designed to create frustration and defeat; to prepare people for a life they can never find and to handicap them in every possible way in attempting to meet new situations in which their adult lives must be led. To a very large extent this is due to the old tradition that only the wisdom of the past was of any value, and therefore education has drawn upon the past for its content and taught the past as the sole dependable guide to the future. Moreover, as we are beginning to realize, the anxieties and guilt feelings of parents, teachers, ministers, and others concerned with the education of the young force them to impose all their fears and needs upon children, adolescents, and young adults, thus burdening them with all the frustrations and defeats of their elders. As the individual grows up these educational experiences become more controlling and coercive, and he meets life with increasing anxiety as his own personal patterns of conduct and all the fears and worries that have been given him by others operate to handicap his efforts to meet the persistent tasks of life which all individuals must face.

These personal difficulties become ever more acute as the individual grows older, especially when he retires or withdraws from active working life. While engaged in the daily round of working he could find some defense or escape from his personal problems, but upon retirement he must face his basic personality difficulties in all their acute form. We hear a great deal about the importance of helping people to solve their personality problems; this is undoubtedly an erroneous view since a little reflection will show us that we cannot solve our personality problems since they are the persistent ways in which we organize our experience, interpret life, and feel toward people. In other words, our personality problems are the inevitable aspects of the private world in which we live and from which we can never escape. For example, Wilder remarks in *The Woman of Andros*, "Most people go through life trying to hide as best they can their consternation that life after all contains no wonderful surprise and the most difficult burden of all is the incommunicability of love." We can, with intelligence and courage, and with some help from others restate our personality problems on different levels of understanding and insight or on what we might say are successive levels of maturity—if we can and do mature.

Thus we see that the persistent perplexities and anxieties with which we have more or less learned to live in our period of life, become the major focus of living in our later years. All the old anxieties, hates, and resentments, all the old compulsions begin to occupy us when we are no longer busy, when we are no longer needed, when we are alone. Moreover, many of the impulses and functional needs which we learned to repress in our early childhood begin to emerge in later life and clamor for expression or release. And so again we may find ourselves confronted with the same difficulties and perplexities as in our adolescence and early childhood.

Perhaps we can understand the situation more clearly if we will realize that the past is not out in some mysterious space, but the past is in us; past experience is a part of us and continues to operate in us in the present just as our mammalian ancestry continues to operate in our organic systems and physiological functions. As we grow older our forgotten childhood revives our memory of childhood experiences, and increases as our memory for recent events fades. Thus we may say that the older individual becomes increasingly preoccupied with his past, especially his early childhood, and increasingly subject to those persistent feelings of anxiety and resentment which he developed in his early life.

When we speak of the older person in the changing social scene we should think, not merely of our changing technology and the various social, economic, and political developments, since these are chiefly the background from which the older person projects his private world like a lantern slide upon a screen. To the extent that this projected private world is increasingly out of focus with the contemporary social life, the older individual will be perplexed and confused. But the major difficulty which each individual faces, especially as he grows older, is within that private world as the persistent conflicts and the emotional distortions and reactions become ever more acute with the passage of years and the almost inevitable frustrations they bring.

We cannot possibly slow down the social changes, indeed certain changes are so long overdue that for the next generation or two we must look forward to even larger reorganizations and changes with possibly considerable violence and disturbance, expressive of the prolonged resistance to these needed readjustments. We may, if we are intelligent, achieve some kind of social order, and strive to synchronize the social changes which at present are so uneven and unbalanced. For the older individual our efforts should be primarily to help him to make the revisions which are necessary because of advancing age and social changes. But what is even more important, we must discover what is taking place inside of him and help him to accept him or herself and come to terms with other individuals and their personalities. In other words, we may say that good social adjustment for the young and for the older individual is primarily a question of how they have been able to assimilate their own past experience and to come to terms with themselves, rather than how they have adjusted to the external, social, economic, and political situation.

Nothing is more pathetic than the poignant spectacle of men and women, sixty, seventy, and over, still driven by the anxieties and ambitions of youth, still torn by the insecurity and guilt of their adolescent years. How many individuals of older years live a life of continual unhappiness and misery because they are dominated by persistent feelings of resentment and hostility, still engaged in fighting the battles of their childhood, against their parents, teachers, against all adults who frustrated them, deprived them, coerced them, and even brutalized and terrorized them. How miserable is that old age in which the individual can find no release from those driving ambitions to get even, to show other people that he is not as bad as he had been told he was in childhood.

With aging, there is the possibility that the pattern of inhibition and repression built up in childhood may be broken through by the impulsive life that has been long buried underneath. Every psychiatrist has had the experience of knowing some man of social, economic, or business standing who has been caught in an action, say a sex offense, which seems perfectly incredible in connection with that individual and incredible to the man himself. These inhibitions that we build up in childhood may begin to slip and lose their cogency of control. Impulse and curiosity break through, to the consternation of the older person, his friends, relatives—and victims. If we think of the private world of the individual as having a greater or less degree of structuralization or form and a greater or less degree of rigidity, these two dimensions might be useful concepts to employ in discussing the private world of the aging individual.

The mental health of the older individual, therefore, is primarily a question of how he can be helped to escape the feeling of insecurity, the loss of confidence in the strange, changing world around him, and develop some feeling of belongingness and worth to others and find some mode of release and expression in activities that bring him a personal satisfaction, as in handicrafts and various occupational activities, the quantity and pace of which can be suited to his skills and strength.

The mental health needs of older persons are more like those of the young child, not because of the popular and false notion that they are childish, but because the same problems become more acute with the years and the need for reassurance, for "whoness" rather than "whatness," returns in full force. As long as we are vigorous and active and can demonstrate our "whatness" and put it over on people, the question of "whoness" is not so important, but as contemporaries fall by the wayside, the question of "whoness" becomes more insistent.

The very young child or baby, coming into a strange and terrifying world, needs support. The older person's sense of confidence in the world is beginning to diminish and he needs reassurance because of the growing discrepancy between his little universe and what is going on outside.

Thus we see that the basic dimensions of the private world of the older person will be the focus of any endeavor to foster better mental health and to provide a design for living that is compatible with their needs and capabilities. The continued sweep of our social and technological processes makes it impossible for the older individual to bring his social situation into conformity with his private world and feelings as frequently occurred in older, simpler communities. Instead, therefore, of the usual pattern of fighting the world, or withdrawing into a sulky retreat from life, our effort should be to help individuals to reorganize their private worlds so that they can live more at peace with themselves and less in conflict with society. To a very large extent this means deliberately planning for our old age, something which individuals rarely do, because they have such strong resistance to even thinking of their later years of life. Until recently only a few individuals did survive, but with the increasing number of older individuals we must try to develop some more systematic program to foster this preparation for later life.

Can we work out a scheme that will make life more happy and less disturbing without seeing clearly that this involves doing something to society as well as to the individual? I am inclined to say that the psychiatric formula that people must "face reality" is susceptible of a gross misuse. It may be a defeatist program and so I should like to base my protest on the use of the term "facing reality." Our task is not to face reality but to try to create a reality that would fit human needs and values. New hope comes with the new culture which is part of the ever-changing historical process. With this viewpoint of correcting reality as much as accepting it, we can agree to the more specific facts about the mental health of old age without being misled into accepting a defeatist attitude.

It is sometimes thought that an older population is necessarily a more conservative one. If old people are unable to achieve a degree of security and peace, they may be rigid as voters, and have a conservative or even reactionary influence on our social life. But the older person is not by nature inclined to be more rigid than the younger. If we allow him to be more active in the community and participate more in the world about him, he may not have to be so conservative. We have not developed the roles for older people to a point that would clarify their many human relationships with family, friends, and others. We need a great many new roles for old people. The book *All Passion Spent* by Victoria Sackville-West tells the story of a woman who has served her husband's political career, but who upon his death prefers to set up life for herself. For the first time in her life she has time to reflect and work out her own plans.

We are not making sufficient demands upon older people. What they want is not idleness and freedom, but an opportunity to do something with their lives that will make them significant. Thornton Wilder says, in *The Woman of Andros,* "We can only be said to be alive in those moments when our hearts are conscious of our treasures." We have to increase the number of such moments for old people.

Until recently we have been inclined to think of health and sanity as something that was mysteriously lost, but today we are beginning to realize that health and sanity must be achieved by meeting the tasks of life more adequately, courageously, and effectively. To the extent that the education of children and adolescents and the growing programs of adult education can and will attempt to help individuals to meet life situations more affectively and realistically, in terms of the new understandings and insights and awarenesses that are now becoming available, we may be able, with mental hygiene and preventive medicine in childhood and adolescence, to build a wiser and happier pattern of life for the older person in the midst of our changing social scene.

We cannot do a great deal for the older person without at the same time doing a great deal for society. One is a reflex of the other. If we have a society that will tolerate the humiliation and degradation of human beings, we will have the personality distortions, intolerances, and cruelties which is the other side of that kind of society. All over the world different societies have given rise to their predominant character structures. If we favor a certain kind of social structure we pay the price in people who cannot make the grade and people who have to be sacrificed. Cultures have been set up that have met more successfully than we have the problem of recognizing the integrity of individuals.

We must find some way of taking into account the increasing number of old people, some way of making the transition from maturity to old age with a minimum of the destruction, wastage, unhappiness, and misery that now obtains so widely. Only when we stress the value of the individual personality will old people come into their own.

THE OLDER PERSON IN THE WORLD OF TODAY—IN THE FAMILY

By Ollie A. Randall *

BASIC to this entire discussion is the question whether we believe the family will continue to be the unit of our society and our democracy or whether we think it one of the institutions doomed to obsolescence as Spengler has called it in his *Decline of the West*. I prefer to regard the family as a structural unit of society which will survive this period of social revolution or evolution we are living through. But I also believe that the family in surviving will undergo very radical changes.

As we look back upon the development of our country, we must be struck by the fact that the tie of kinship has operated to help form the family into a kind of economic unit, made up of individuals who otherwise might have found it impossible to remain in the same functioning group. The past several generations have seen rapid and startling changes in this respect, since the industrial revolution had done away with the necessity or even possibility of any one family's being its own self-contained unit. Though one can still cite instances outside the urban areas of families in which several generations continue to live together because they are carrying on this old tradition of "family." The large family mansions in which it was expected that the older people would continue to live, with the younger generations joining them in different degrees of independence, or dependence, is familiar to us in real life as well as in fiction. But it is a phenomenon rapidly disappearing today because of industrial and social factors. Those working with older people in the crowded city find the situation in which it is physi-

* Assistant Director, Special Services Division, Community Service Society of New York.

cally possible for this plan of living to obtain to be practically non-existent.

It seems that while we can intellectually accept the fact that as a practical or physical measure several generations cannot easily arrange to live together, there is a distinct lag between this acceptance and any change in attitude toward what we can or do accept in the matter of family relationships. Obviously, this is because the family is a group of persons whose relationship is recognized by themselves as being based not upon economic reasons but upon the ties of kinship and affection and the intangible emotional and spiritual ties whose strength is far greater than any other.

We find ourselves, then, struggling with living arrangements entered into because actually "blood is thicker than water." Kinship still carries with it responsibilities which often, when assumed by our present-day generations result only in an unworkable plan and in unhappiness for everyone concerned. We may not be able to alter our definition of what a family is, but we can change our ideas of what is a natural living arrangement for members of a family if the individuals who compose it are to be happy and self-sufficient persons in the community.

This is by no means so simple as it sounds. For we have had as an integral part of our cultural background a philosophy of living which imposes on the family the task of caring for the aged and infirm. Too abrupt a change of anything which is woven so closely into the fabric of our habit of thought and of living is a painful process—and, perhaps, an undesirable one.

As a result of depressions and a consequent shift of social responsibility for the support of an increasing population of elderly people, events are moving much more rapidly than is our thinking about these events, at least in individual situations. For instance, the gap between the governmental program of support, with the attendant individualization of the family, and any real reflection of it in the legislation providing for old age assistance is evidenced by the present provisions for the support by legally responsible relatives. This in many instances of practice is not consonant with the intent of the law but stems directly from our age-old attitude toward family relationships. In a strict interpretation of the law, its original purpose is often defeated, and the effect upon family life may be most unfortunate.

I am not advocating at this time any liberalization of the law either for children or for parents and grandparents in the matter of the responsibility for support, for we must still count upon the social force of family ties to balance the real limitations of tax resources for meeting the actual economic job of taking care of our old people. But in the demand that this be done—particularly when the demand is a legal one—I find the basis for much of the unhappiness for both the old and the young who are living together in family settings.

I recall hearing Dr. Hartwell say in a lecture that "the goal of mental hygiene is to help the individual to live his life in all age periods—from beginning to end—in a way that will be most acceptable and pleasant to himself and most acceptable and useful to others." This is also the goal of those who are working with elderly people in family groups, and the latter have a challenge in their efforts to achieve their objective far greater than that faced by those working at other age levels.

Now I believe that if this goal is reached for the elderly person or persons, it is very often reached as a by-product or by a very natural process for the other members of the family. The challenge lies in the fact that we don't always realize that we need to be more careful, more understanding, and to work harder with old people because they are the individuals whose "psychological welfare," as Dr. Lawton has put it, "is more neglected than that of any other group of persons."

Recently I heard a well-trained social worker say that those in family work had forgotten that essential to a family are the children in it, and perhaps we should "rediscover" the child if we are to preserve the family as a democratic unit. I wanted to remind her and others that we should also in our social work consciousness "discover" the older person or persons in the family, who are for purposes of family work merely counted "among those present," but whose interests are almost always discounted in favor of those of others—persons presumably more important in the scheme of living.

Is there anything really new in the relation of an older generation to a younger one? It seems to me that it is as old as our knowledge of man. But perhaps we can also agree that the difficulties surrounding that relationship have been definitely aggravated by the social and economic changes of recent years, especially in urban centers.

While living in the country is today both physically easier and more comfortable and economically more complex than it was fifty years ago—owing to marketing and transportation facilities which bring the outside world to the door—it is still far from being as complex and complicated as life in the city. What we can do about reducing or removing the difficulties is one problem when the old person and his family live in the country and an entirely different one when they live in the city.

Family relationships may be divided into three classifications. In all the years I have worked with elderly people each situation appears to be a variation of one of these basic three.

First, there are the countless families in which the old and the young work out their living plans happily, or at least to their mutual satisfaction, though we are apt to think otherwise because the majority of the situations which come to our attention do not fall in this group. If this isn't so, then our population figures and estimates are decidedly askew.

The second group are those families in which the difficulties of getting along are greater for the older people, whether for economic, social, or emotional reasons. Many times, if the economic strain could be removed, members of this group would be included in the first group, as the work of the old age assistance program so conclusively demonstrates.

In the third group are the families in which the difficulties of working out acceptable relationships are greater for the younger generations. Those who have made the care of the aged their major interest, might well be reminded occasionally, that we must not lose sight of the fact that we may satisfy the needs and desires of the older person at too great a cost to the younger people in the situation.

In New York City we cannot, in considering the mental health or well being of elderly people, quite so cavalierly dismiss the economic factor as does Mr. Frank in his discussion. Quite understandably, in order to make his points of individual adjustment, he had to disregard extraneous considerations such as environmental and economic factors. But for a total picture of what enters into either making or breaking down mental health we must remember that many family difficulties arise from financial stringency. With that, too, we must remember the growing individualization of the family, to which continued city life under marginal or moderate income may possibly contribute by making affectional ties less binding than they would be in rural life under similar limitations.

There is little to discuss in the first group I have mentioned, although it is essential if we are to have a sense of balance to know that satisfactory relationships exist. We should also study these carefully when we have the opportunity, in order to discover, if we can, what are the factors which bring about success in family living. This is as necessary as continually focusing our attention upon those situations in which apparent failure exists.

Even in the "satisfactory" situations, it is rather common to have elderly people come for advice when they are convinced that some shift on their part will be helpful either to them or to their children or relatives, though there may be no difficulty apparent on the surface of things.

There is the older person who has had a full life with much responsibility, who has the ability to be very rational about the changes which come with the years. Yet such a person may find the life of security with children or younger relatives, whether it be dependent or independent, far from being wholly satisfying. I am thinking particularly of individuals whom I nominate to myself as persons of lost identity—or, rather, of a changed identity. They are not quite in the position of Philip Nolan in "The Man without a Country," but they are often persons without a past which has anything to do with the present in which they are living.

Such a woman came to see me the other day. On the face of it,

Mrs. Stone would be the last person in the world one would expect to look for suggestions regarding an old age home to which she might go. But as I talked with her, I realized that her visit was the result of a very logical conclusion. Mrs. Stone was a woman in her late sixties, well set-up, beautifully groomed and fashionably dressed in excellent taste, intelligent, and possessing a most unusual sense of humor and a fund of common sense beyond that which most of us have. She was a widow, whose resources, like those of so many others in these years, disappeared through the poor judgment of the executors of her husband's estate. She could find no real fault with them, she admitted, for after all, in the late twenties and the early thirties they were in a numerous and high company, and there was, she said, no reason for her to expect them to be endowed with a superhuman business acumen with regard to her securities.

Mrs. Stone had no children, but she had two nephews and a niece, living in different cities and in different parts of the country. Each was married and comfortably enough situated to be able to provide her with a home. But what was more important, each was very fond of her and eager to have her. Mrs. Stone in her own affluent days had an excellent flair and skill in interior decoration, although she had never been commercially engaged in that occupation. She therefore found herself extremely useful and busy in their homes—devising color and decorative schemes, making curtains, slip covers and so on, so that she had a satisfaction in realizing that her care was in no sense a total loss to them. She was welcome socially in their homes, and was invited to share in the social activities of the family. Each had, however, established his home in a city in which she had never lived or known anyone in her younger days, or when she might have been received as Judge Stone's wife of Columbus, Ohio.

As she put it, "In each home I am 'John's Aunt Louise,' or 'May's Aunt Louise'—never Mrs. Stone of Columbus with a background and life of my own. I meet no one who knows me for myself, and I honestly believe I'd be happier in a home with other people of my own age, who accept me for myself as myself, even though they didn't know me earlier, than to go on living as I do now. My nephew won't be able to understand why I want to make this application, for he has a place for me and will give me a small allowance, but I hoped you might understand."

Mrs. Stone will, I am sure, be able to work out a philosophy which will help her, but in it she needs the help of other members of the family. Her consideration for them makes it impossible for her at this time to let them know that she had any cause for dissatisfaction or discontent, for she appreciates fully their fondness for her and their acceptance of responsibility for her, which she knows stems from both genuine affection and their attitude toward family ties. I believe she will work through the situation herself and find a new "identity."

In the meantime, Mrs. Stone's application for residence in Ward Manor has been accepted. The final decision, however, when we get it, will be determined by a careful balance of what is socially desirable for Mrs. Stone at the time, against what may be economically and socially necessary for others who are also awaiting admission. If our resources were ideally adequate, individuals like Mrs. Stone who want to be part of a group, ought to be able to choose the kind of arrangement they wish, but with the pressure of demands from those who are actually in financial or physical need of the protection which group living in a home provides, it may not be possible to meet this kind of a situation in the near future. She is not in any sense eligible for support from public funds, because of the ability and willingness of her family to support her, nor is her family financially able to set her up in independent living, even though Mrs. Stone and her relatives were ready to accept such a plan. The hope for her lies in her own good sense and the help which some person or agency can give her in developing a plan in which she achieves an individuality apart from that of being "Charley's Aunt."

If I may indulge in a bit of personal experience I should like to comment on a situation I have watched in my own family. For it is only by understanding all that goes into this change that we can arrive at more satisfying solutions than might otherwise be possible.

For ten years I have watched my own mother making the very carefully concealed change in status and identity from being Mrs.

Randall, a person of substance in her own community, to that of being a daughter's mother in four or five strange communities, a very especially loved grandmother, or a more-than-welcome mother-in-law. She is a person whom we want very much to have in our homes, so that there results among us a good-natured rivalry in our bidding for her visits to us. The best solution which we have been able to reach since the death of my father and the selling of the large family place has been for her to have a place of her own with each of us.

All her life, from the early days in the Middle West as the eldest in a large pioneer family, through the days of our youth, when she was the responsible head of our family—in which there lived not only our immediate family but, in true New England fashion, my great-grandmother, my grandparents, and two great-aunts,—she has been a member of a large family group, so that living alone is today a disastrous experience for her each time she tries it when the urge for a place of her own comes upon her. Throughout these years the adaptation to the demands of several generations—in her words the lesson of "the two bears, bear and forbear"—have today made it possible for her to fit quietly into the family life of each home and keep herself busily occupied and so useful that she is a real loss when she moves on.

Of course my mother's financial independence contributes greatly to her ability to adjust. Yet through it all runs the fact that to our friends her identity is one that relates only to us and that her personality—the sum total of experiences of her life which have gone into making that personality—is meaningful only to us and is given very little thought by anyone other than ourselves. Yet, what interests me is that being deprived of the status to which she has been accustomed and an identity of her own, apart from that of being our mother, her habits of life are making it possible for her to accept the role which circumstances have brought her in old age. What is especially valuable to her now is the early pioneer training of taking things as they come and making the best of them without too much grumbling. Were it not for that, there are in such a situation the very elements which bring us to the next classification

—families in which relationships are difficult for the older person or persons for any number of reasons.

As I look back over the twenty-five years in which I have talked with older people about their difficulties I am inclined to conclude that those in which adjustments were needed for the older and those needed for the sake of the younger members of the family are about even in number, and, as I have said before, the benefits of such change are apt to fall "like the gentle rain from heaven" about evenly upon the two groups, though I can only claim to have been guided by the facts as we have them rather than by the facts as they are.

We are familiar with the old lady or old gentleman who comes to us with the story that the daughter-in-law (or often the son-in-law) doesn't wish to continue to provide a home and something must be done. Nearly always, in New York City at any rate, because of limited space and limited income, a change is the best method and often the simplest method of achieving harmony, although this is a generalization which is not always true, for there are as many kinds of causes as there are cases. The conflict between generations is historic, and while education over the years may help us to understand and modify the conflict, it never will be simple to resolve the conflict by a purely intellectual approach because emotional reactions are unpredictable.

I recall very clearly the old gentleman, about eighty years of age, physically well, mentally alert, gentle, quiet, unobtrusive, but still possessing a certain amount of initiative so far as his own interests were concerned, who came to us seeking a place in a home for the aged for himself. Mr. Bennett told us he was living in the home of a son, who had several children of the "teen" age of whom he was apparently very fond. And one of them, a boy, evidently found in his grandfather a very companionable person. Yet the old man knew he wasn't wanted, because, as he put it, he occupied a room on the third floor which his daughter-in-law wanted for her son. The family wasn't rich but they could provide for him, and Mr. Bennett's son was willing to do so with the help of a brother and sister. There was no prospect of an immediate vacancy in the home, and with this explained an application was accepted.

However, when the application was returned, it was discovered that the old gentleman had a wife who was residing with a third son in another town. Investigation later brought out some very illuminating facts.

Mr. Bennett, when his four children were young, had left his family for parts unknown. This he had done because he couldn't seem to meet his obligations, either to his own satisfaction or that of his wife. Mrs. Bennett, a more energetic person, took over the support of the children, which she accomplished by dint of hard work of all kinds. She was successful, for she bought a house and paid for it, gave her sons and daughters fairly good educations, with of course, self-help on their part as they grew up. Years later, when each had married and set up his or her own home, and the mother could no longer be active, the father returned to the family rooftree, penniless, and unable to find or to keep work. The children, true to the British tradition of their family background, accepted the financial responsibility for him as a filial duty, but there was no affection in the gesture. There was, very understandably, a certain amount of resentment of his expectation of support from them after the years of his desertion, not only of them, but most especially of their mother.

She was willing to greet and meet her husband in a friendly fashion, but she refused to live in the same house with him. Therefore, the family had compromised on a joint financial support which meant making available room and board and clothing with a minimum of sacrifice on their part and a place for him in the home of one of them in which he knew he was none too welcome. There was enough income in the family to provide with little difficulty for the financial requirements of admission to a private home for the aged, but not one of the children would make it available even though they, as well as he, might have been much happier and more comfortable and the arrangement might ultimately have proved to be less expensive than the one they were carrying out.

No private home would accept Mr. Bennett unless these requirements were met (and some would not even then), since it was plainly possible to meet them. Nor could the old gentleman be received in a public almshouse which would provide the impersonal congregate living he was seeking, because of this same ability on the part of the family to provide material support.

Mr. Bennett was then condemned to an unhappy existence in which he was bearing the brunt of his daughter-in-law's resentment of what he was taking from her son, but in which he was reaping the harvest from his early shirking of family responsibility. The younger generation were equally applying, with a certain amount of satisfaction, punitive measures in their unwillingness to make it possible for him to take up residence in the kind of living in which he would have been more at home because of long years of knocking around from pillar to post. With no justification of the old man's actions, but accepting his earlier life as fact, with some effort to understand the reasons underlying the fact, I believe it would have been better planning for the individual old person, the family, and the community to have succeeded in persuading the children to arrange for his placement in an institution in which he could have been one of a large group and could have made his contribution of "odd jobs," on which he had supported himself through the years.

Mr. Bennett's pattern of daily life and relationships with others throughout a great many years had been impersonal and simple, and a continuation of it would appear to be conducive to less emotional strain and family friction. His major mistake in working out his own problem when the joblessness of age came upon him had probably been his yielding to some deep-seated urge to see his family. One might guess that he had always been very fond of them, but that his own general ineffectiveness pitted against his wife's very strenuous capability had been too much for him and he had not been able "to take it" as his son said.

But once Mr. Bennett was reunited with the family, he destroyed the possibility of receiving any community support. I am not arguing that he should have had it. Our regret was that there were not time and resources for attempting to help the family work out a plan which might have meant more happiness or contentment for the old person. Whenever any situation comes to our attention, it is important (or rather it strikes me anew how essential it is) in order to be helpful to elderly people to have more information about them, both from themselves and from others, than for any other age group. What they have been like in their earlier years, or as children, how they have conducted themselves in their families and in their communities adds immeasurably to our effectiveness in working out any plan with them or for them.

For example, there is the case of elderly Mrs. Snow, who had been born and brought up in the country in very humble circumstances. Always there had been enough, in a way, so that she and her family had preserved their dignity by self-support, but with little or no margin. The mother always was the accepted head of the family, for the father and husband was not much of a manager, although he worked hard as a gardener on a large estate. After the death of her husband, Mrs. Snow had very little cash, just as all through her life. With no near relatives in the country who would or could have her with them, she came to the city to live with a married daughter. The latter did not quarrel with this plan because she accepted it as her duty, even though at the time her home was crowded, for not only did her own children live there but one son had married and brought his young wife into the home. The old lady, moreover, was handicapped by very poor eyesight as well as by unfamiliarity with the neighborhood and had to stay indoors most of the time.

Friction was inevitable, and yet Mrs. Snow's record in the country as a neighbor, a worker, and a mother was a creditable one. She was crude and simple, but sternly Puritanical in her attitude toward family life and the duty of one's children toward their own. After a fairly exhaustive study of the family needs, it was decided that the mother—or grandmother—faced what for her was a pretty hard situation, and that the family friction between generations was the direct result of very crowded living conditions and limited income. A final source of conflict was the widely divergent attitudes of the two and three generations, one from the country and one from the present-day city, toward family, moral, and economic standards.

The daughter was genuinely anxious to do what could be done, but was torn between the so-called respectability of the old age assistance grant for her mother, whose physical limitations made it hard for her to get along in the city, and residence in a home for the aged in the country where all their former friends and neighbors would know that she had "put her mother away." The mother finally decided the matter for herself by choosing the home in the country. There Mrs. Snow has found a certain measure of contentment, because she is in familiar surroundings; and there is a certain freedom of activity because of the fact that she is out of the city; but she has also proved herself to be a very stubborn old lady. Her daughter now admits reluctantly that her mother was always the one at home who "told everyone else what to do and when to do it" and the yielding habit is so strong with this daughter, herself now a grandmother, that she will make any sacrifice rather than raise an issue with her mother over anything at all.

Though it took a great deal of time, patience, effort, and devious maneuvering to consummate the arrangement finally planned for Mrs. Snow, it is the best for all concerned. The action taken to make the old lady more comfortable has proved to be even more in the interest of the rest of the family. For it has lessened their responsibility and has taken out of the family a rather dominating old lady, who couldn't give up her lifelong habit of telling the members of the family what they should do.

Loss of status of this kind in family groups is one of the greatest deprivations which old people face. So few seem to learn the lesson that to be a consultative and directional force rather than a dictatorial one carries with it often a greater dignity and a really greater power or importance. People like Grandmother Whiteoak in *Jalna* are pleasanter folks to meet in fiction than in one's daily life. Matriarchs are dramatic when one is reading about them, but they are extremely hard to live with.

Family loss of status is generally associated with either a lessening or a total cessation of earning capacity or of economic power. However, it may also be the result of the necessity of living in unfamiliar or a very much changed environment. If I may be permitted another personal illustration, I can cite an incident that pointed this up for me very clearly.

Several years ago we suffered here in the East a major cataclysm in the form of a severe hurricane which caused a great deal of damage to our home place, a remote and simple farm in a rural section of Rhode Island. As a result, for days and weeks we had to carry on under very primitive conditions without any of the so-called improvements which we had recently put into the house and to which we have all become so thoroughly accustomed. There was no running water or electricity; there was difficulty in getting food and in keeping it once you got it; and there were all sorts of makeshifts necessary to live, to say nothing of making the repairs to damaged buildings and land around the house.

In our family group at the time was an elderly woman, an old family retainer who had been a kind of legacy with the farm and who had never in all her seventy-six years moved farther than twenty-five miles away from the valley. With us also at the time was my mother, who had all her early life lived in a pioneer family in the West. These women met the emergency with great ease and took the lead in planning just how we would get along without gas, running water, light, telephone, refrigeration. The rest of us, all adults, were less than children in this simple life. The way these women assumed leadership and the way we let them do so was an illuminating experience to me. They had the feeling they were being exceptionally useful, and that they could carry a job to a conclusion. Once more they were persons to whom others turned for advice and help. This worked wonders for those two women, not only in their attitude toward the situation and to us, but in their physical ability to work without fatigue, or at least fatigue of which they complained or were even conscious. What would once have exhausted them was now amusing. Here was an absolute demonstration of the way older people need a continuation of a former status which is recognized by others if there is to be a wholesome normal amount of contentment on their part as well as greater degree of physical well-being.

But to return to the economic situation and its effect on status and relationships, I should like to mention the unfailing gullibility of human nature as evidenced by the number of older people who still have faith that by turning over all their real and other property in a lump sum to some member of the family they can be in return guaranteed support for life. Many old people have taken this means for providing for their future without anticipating the resultant difficulties through changed conditions and attitudes. Through the fact that they are deprived of the only thing which may have made their presence in a family tolerable on any basis, they suffer agonies of disillusionment and deflated ego, painful at any time for anyone, but unusually so for old people with no opportunity for retrenchment or reinstatement. As one old lady said to me the other day, "What a fool I've been! And even the government doesn't want to support fools!"

Such misunderstanding need not always nor does it usually arise out of bad intent or dishonesty on the part of the younger generation. It often is due to the fact that the younger people are ignorant of the exaggerated idea that the old people may have of the value of their property, either real or cash, and the older person's lack of understanding of what it may accomplish in a new and very complex world. When money or property is turned over to someone else to manage, with the definite promise of continued support as a factor in the transaction, the seed has been planted of an ultimate misunderstanding which can disrupt a family completely, especially as few legal documents are drawn up in such contracts because they are family matters. We know too that even when such agreements are made in genuinely legal fashion between institutions and individuals there is the same attitude. The old person frequently is heard to express the feeling that he has paid far too dearly for the care he is receiving, ignoring the fact that for an equivalent sum of money paid to any insurance company he would receive a much lesser degree of security than he expects either from his family or from a home for the aged. Of course, we must realize all that has gone into the accumulation of the possessions, what they must have meant in the lives of the old people, and what relinquishing possessions does in reducing the individual's sense of importance.

The factor which makes for the greatest misunderstandings or strain between the generations is illness, either physical or mental. The acuteness of the difficulty is in no way related to the acuteness of the illness—if anything, it is apt to be in inverse ratio to it. In emergencies, even the least capable of us find some way of measuring up to the demands of the occasion, and all of us are continually being surprised by the resourcefulness exhibited in families when a supreme need arises.

But when the illness is of the chronic type—long drawn out, demanding steady, unremitting service, both in terms of medical and personal care, few families of limited means or limited quarters can continue indefinitely on the high level of emergent demands. Nothing taxes one's patience more than caring day in, day out, for the needs of the old person whose chances of being restored to health are slight or non-existent but whose daily needs continue on the same, if not on an increasingly demanding, level. This is also true in those cases of mild mental affliction—which include loss of memory, lack of orientation, forms of suspiciousness which may develop into what we speak of as a persecution complex, and confusion—which often create intolerable disorder in the household and for which institutional care is not available or may not even be desirable. No matter how well one knows that this is no fault of the individual, there are bound to be moments when one's nerves are frayed, and irritability and exasperation result in unhappiness for all concerned. This is particularly true in families containing three generations, where the younger members are denied what we call a normal social life in the home because of the disturbed old person.

It is in situations of this kind that we must make an attempt at what workers call "manipulation of environment" and what in simpler terminology I call finding a new living arrangement for the old person. And as usual, when this kind of change seems most eminently suitable it is often the hardest thing to do, either because the facilities are not easily available or because the family cannot accept the idea or because the old person cannot be persuaded that a change is desirable. I might point out that at times when such a change seems indicated, the results of moving an old person without his consent have often justified such a procedure, for he is often much happier and more comfortable than before.

Often it is for the sake of the family unit itself—or the younger members of it—that the older people ought to be placed in another setting. I recall very vividly the case of one man and woman with three very promising young children from five to eleven years of age. The man was a high school principal in a small town, so that the salary was not large, but the cultural advantages were excellent and the family enjoyed a happy place in the community. A short time ago, the woman's mother, a person of Swedish birth, who had not been in the home before and who found it hard to be happy in the cultural pattern of the family, was taken very ill and came to stay with them. The daughter, loyal to a very great degree, and with a very high sense of responsibility to her mother which her husband approved, had all the best medical advice she could obtain. The local physicians advised consultation with several very expensive surgeons from a city some distance away, and the daughter authorized this, although it meant mortgaging to the hilt every bit of property the family had. After the consultation, an operation was advised and this further strained the resources of the family, for it necessitated more borrowing.

Now the mother is a chronic invalid in the home; the family is not going to get out of debt contracted for at least fifteen years; and those are critical years for the young people. Most persons would rightly conclude that this was all unwise, and the judgment of the family very poor. But how does one answer a daughter who says with a harried and worried look, "But I simply had to have the best for my mother, and that was the only way I could be sure I'd be giving her a chance to live."

Were this daughter's values mixed when she sacrificed the possibility of good education and equipment of the young for the present comfort and support of her elderly mother, whose presence in the home not only disrupted household routine and produced actual discomfort but caused all their other difficulties? Isn't this the question which we encounter so often in trying to work out methods of establishing eligibility for old age assistance and in trying to determine the desirability of separate maintenance in a home for the aged, or in some other plan for the old people?

I confess to being quite baffled, for in it is bound up the whole question of responsibility of tax payers who themselves cannot in many instances arrange for themselves the changes in their own families which we believe to be desirable for applicants for the grant, or for admission to our homes for the aged. But I believe that for the sake of the old people and the other members of the family we ought to weigh the social considerations more heavily than we now do when arriving at our decisions.

Recently, I was presented with this family situation. There was an elderly man of eighty-four and his wife of seventy-six, neither one well and yet neither one very ill. They had brought up five children, who were all married with their own children and grandchildren. Not any one of the families was really "well off," but one or two were more comfortable than the others. However, in each of these homes were "in-laws" who refused to take any responsibility for the old people, financial or otherwise. Each one of the children on being interviewed expressed a genuine interest in the old folks, and a willingness to help, but not one would assume entire responsibility for them, because each was convinced it was something they should all share.

Evidently those less well off were jealous of those better off. There was constant bickering among them because of this as well as because of the misunderstanding which arose out of the disposition of a small piece of property which the old people once had had. A number of conferences with the family, in which their native good sense was invariably evident, except when it came to the subject of money, confirmed the truth of the old saying, "A mother can support five sons, but five sons cannot support a mother."

The Division of Old Age Assistance finally decided that the

old people were eligible for help and that for their sake some permanent plan for their care should be made which would be acceptable to everyone. The Old Age Assistance grant was paid to them in the home of a married daughter. But the family quarrel still continued, for the children with small cash incomes all exaggerated the possibilities of regular income going to the daughter. It was therefore deemed best that the old couple enter a private home for the aged, and that there should be a sharing of the responsibility for meeting the small personal expenses of the old folks. The old people love the present arrangement, for they have their own room. Now when they and their children see each other, money is not the only subject of discussion. For the present, at least, they are all friends.

We must remember that in this family money never was plentiful or easy to get, although no one ever actually lacked physical or material comfort. Therefore, the intense feeling over what seems a relatively small amount was understandable, and had to be regarded as carefully as though it were larger. In this instance, it seemed equally desirable for the children, the grandchildren (who were genuinely fond of their grandparents), and the older people themselves, to see that the latter got separate living arrangements. The old people have found themselves and are living a happy, quiet existence so far as their personal satisfaction is concerned.

One could say a good deal about what happens in homes where there are very young children, and where there is a conflict in methods of child care and training, and of running a household. The matter of training of children is apt to be dynamite in most homes unless there is both firmness on the one hand and restraint on the other.

I remember one little girl about seven who came one day with her mother to see me about a great-aunt who was being considered for Ward Manor. Said aunt must have been a disturbing personality in the home, because of a different racial background and a long life of living alone before trying to carry on in the home of a nephew who had married an American woman. The little girl at first refused to come into my room, but finally she peeked around the corner of the office and her consternation was most amusing. Looking at me with wide-open eyes, she said to her mother in most surprised tones, "But mummy, how could Miss Randall look like that? I don't see how anybody would want Auntie to come to live with her unless she was old and gray haired, and horrid and cross!" Yet Auntie proved to be a satisfactory member of a family group at Ward Manor, because the group was all adult and there were no elements of personal responsibility for her.

We want the relationships between the generations in a family such that one's idea of each is pleasant. If family life fostered an early belief that old age is not only welcome to the old person but to other members of the family, growing old might be an easier process for all of us. I think of the old folks of our family not so much as being merely old, but just as being always there, of having a kind of permanent quality which gave all of us a sense of stability some of which seemed to leave with them when they went from us. The present world situation robs us of that because the old people as individuals have themselves been deprived of any such sense of stability.

In a family, the mental health or the happiness of the old person is one part of the sum total of happiness for all the members of the family. With the growing individualization of the family, whether it consists of adults and children or all adults, a better adjustment for all may often be achieved by separating the generations rather than by clinging to our old ideas of family living. We may be forced to discard our ideas of a dynasty as a family, and think of it for purposes of living as only the immediate family of parents and children while the children are growing into adulthood.

"Life with Father" is admittedly a very different thing today for so many reasons that they cannot be enumerated. Yet, I am sure we want to retain for family living those characteristics which as human beings we need at any age and which we still find in a family more easily than elsewhere—love, companionship, understanding, tolerance, and sympathy, which we can still expect more directly and with more assurance from members of our own family or of our "own blood" than elsewhere.

But I am equally sure that we must face a modification of our ideas of family living as we have known it, and as we very often think it should be today. We are moving into an era when going to live with old folks, or having the old folks come to live with us will be difficult to achieve with equal satisfaction to all the persons involved. I say this, aware that some years ago those working with old people were accused of being kind but not intelligent and that today we are told we are over-protecting the old people—another way of saying the same thing.

What I hope we can do in the future is to be kind *and* intelligent, protective *and* helpful, and at the same time stimulating to a fuller personal life for elderly people, which should include family life in its fullest meaning—real satisfaction derived from it no matter what its plan for each participant.

PHYSICAL CHANGES IN OLD AGE AND THEIR EFFECTS UPON MENTAL ATTITUDES

By Lewellys F. Barker *

WHY DOES MAN GROW OLD AND DIE?

DURING the millions of years since living creatures began to exist on the earth, animals of many varieties have slowly developed from the earlier simpler forms to the mammalian types culminating in man. Compared with the limitations of lower animals, the widely extended activities of thought, feeling, and action of human beings have made possible what we know as modern civilization with its physical and material comforts, its intellectual and emotional interests, its opportunities for personal freedom, its economic organization, its social institutions, its expansion of knowledge and power, its political relationship (local, national, and international), its achievements in the realms of art, literature, and science, and its creation of ethical values—a development that is truly astounding.

But the specialization of function that has permitted a greater richness of life carries with it its own penalty, for the reciprocal interdependence of the cells, tissues, and organs is accompanied inevitably by an aging ,process, and ultimately each human organism must die, no matter how good its heredity has been nor how favorable the environment in which it has lived. Though it is true that life expectancy for man has been greatly increased, especially in our own time, this increase has been due mainly to the prevention of mortality in infants, children, and younger people through the prevention and cure of infectious diseases, advances in surgery, bet-

* Professor Emeritus of Medicine, Johns Hopkins Medical School, Baltimore.

ter general hygiene, and growth in our knowledge of nutrition. The increased life expectancy has been chiefly for the young; the gain for persons over fifty has been only slight in the past century, and life expectancy after the age of sixty has recently been diminishing. Many doubt if average longevity can be made to exceed sixty, unless eugenic practices should come to be more generally adopted.

The maximal span of life for higher organisms is roughly five times the number of years required for development to maturity—for man say five times twenty-one, or 105. Extremely few persons, even among those of good inheritance living in the most favorable environment, exceed or even reach this age. There have, it is true, been a few notable exceptions. The case of the Dane C. J. Drakenberg is most often referred to; it was claimed that he had reached his 146th year when he died in 1772. Another instance is the one Kucynski described who was at least 109 years old when he died. That a few people have lived to be over a hundred years old is undoubtedly true, but there have not been many nor do I believe that there ever will be many, despite the more sanguine prophecies of certain Moscow investigators.

It should not be forgotten that until the age of seventy people like to be considered younger than they really are, but that very old people may have an opposite tendency and may lay claim to a greater longevity than they have in reality enjoyed. We should be sceptical, therefore, of reports of extreme longevity until they have been carefully tested as to their reliability. Nascher once paid a visit to a man in Kentucky who was said to be "the oldest living human being"; though he was reputed to be 118 years or older, Nascher found on careful study that he could not have been more than 98!

Man is subject to the biological laws that govern other higher animals; he is born, undergoes development to maturity, normally reproduces his kind, may pass through middle life to senescence, but, in time, after he has fulfilled his fundamental biological functions, must inexorably die. During his lifetime many "minor involutions" occur in his body—the branchial clefts during foetal life, the thymus at puberty, the tonsils during middle age; but, when he lives long, he must finally undergo the "major involution" that ends in his death. The "minor involutions" are desirable for the good of the individual, the "major involution" is necessary for the good of the human race. As Goethe said, "Death is Nature's device for securing abundant life."

The slow transformation of a human being, but with continuance of personality from his birth to his death, through the weakness of infancy, the impetuosity of youth, the seriousness of middle age, and the ripeness of old age can be represented in the form of a graph. Metabolism begins to diminish soon after birth, the musculature reaches its maximum of functional capacity at about the age of thirty, the genital functions begin to decline in middle life and the intellectual functions at sixty or later. The slowness of the change is apt to give the false impression of permanent duration.

But as a matter of fact, the curve of the graph is predetermined by the constitution of the germ plasm at the moment the human ovum is fertilized by the sperm cell; as James S. McLester figuratively puts it, "the arc of the bullet is determined by the charge it receives before it leaves the muzzle." Life can be ended prematurely, of course, by disease or violence, but aside from these it pursues the path that is determined for it by the inherent qualities of the genes from which it starts. Longevity is exquisitely hereditary: the best insurance of long personal existence is derivation from long-lived ancestors.

PHYSIOLOGICAL AND PATHOLOGICAL OLD AGE

In "physiological" or "natural" old age, there is a gradual process of cell atrophy and a relative increase in the supporting tissues of the bodily organs. The physical infirmities of later life have been manifoldly described through the centuries both by laymen and by medical men. The latter are very familiar with the early failure of accommodation in the eyes, the graying of the hair, the loss of teeth, the diminution of sex desire and potency, the increased fatigability, the stiffening of the joints, the flabbiness of the muscles, the wrinkling of the skin, the white zone at the periphery of the cornea, the thickening and calcification of the arteries, the shortness of breath on exertion, the slowing of digestion, the tendency to constipation and hemorrhoids, the enlargement of the prostate with difficulty in starting the flow of urine, the diminution of the endocrine functions, and the changes in the gait and in muscular coordination.

Along with these physical changes, slight mental disturbances become manifest. There is forgetfulness of names, lack of receptivity to new ideas with increasing tendency to conservatism, beginning loss of memory for recent events, difficulty of sustained attention and concentration, increased egocentricity, stubbornness, and tendency to suspicion, as well as increased irritability and emotionalism.

But despite all these physical and mental infirmities, the old may still enjoy life. All normal people desire long life provided there is not too much disturbance of bodily and mental health. You may recall Talleyrand's witty paradoxical statement, "Everybody wants to live long, but nobody wants to be old."

Physiological old age depends in the main upon the constitution that is inherited, though the manner of life that has been led and the environmental factors to which a person has been exposed also play a part. Adam in *As You Like It* looked old but was still strong and lusty; Shakespeare thought that this was due to the fact that in youth he had lived hygienically, never wooing "the means of weakness and debility"; his age was described as a "lusty winter, frosty but kindly."

Fortunately, in many people who attain to physiological old age, the intellectual, artistic, and spiritual faculties are long retained; one need only be reminded of Sophocles, who wrote his *Oedipus* when he was 90; of Titian, who produced his masterpiece at the age of 85 and lived to be 99; of Benjamin Franklin, who was fruitfully active until the age of 82; of Oliver Wendell Holmes, who at 85 wrote his fascinating *Over the Tea Cups* and of Cardinal Gibbons, who in 1919 published an article entitled "Why I Am Well at Eighty." The two Flexner brothers are good contemporary examples of the retainment of mental ability in physiological senescence, for Abraham Flexner, now 75, recently published an outstanding autobiography, and his older brother Simon Flexner, now over 78, just completed his life of the late Dr. William H. Welch.

But *pathological* old age is an entirely different affair. It is something that all who know about it must ardently hope to escape, for none of us wants to be a serious burden either to himself or to others. Severe bodily diseases may make later life almost intolerable and exert most depressing mental effects upon such oldsters. Even worse are the presenile and senile psychoses with their catastrophic effects upon the personalities of those who suffer from them.

PHYSICAL CHANGES AND MENTAL ATTITUDES IN SIMPLE SENILE DEMENTIA

From 10 to 15 percent of admission to hospitals for the insane are cases of simple dementia. The disorder begins with narrowing of the range of interests, forgetfulness, and dulling of the emotional reactions, symptoms like those that occur in physiological senescence. But in senile dementia the changes occur more rapidly and reach a higher degree of intensity. The disturbances of memory are progressive from the memory of recent events to that of more remote occurrences. This loss of memory may take place so schematically that one can sometimes determine the decade to which it reaches back. (Bleuler). Falsifications of memory are frequent, earlier experiences being inexactly reproduced; for example, one man of eighty insisted that he was only eighteen. The recording faculty is markedly disturbed; we notice faulty attention, difficulty of concentration, slowing of perception, and faulty associational processes. Gaps of memory are often filled up by silly confabulations. In conversation, the thread of the discourse is often lost; the attention may sometimes be too easily deflected, whereas at other times the old adhere tenaciously to certain definite thoughts from which they cannot be pried loose.

Severe disturbances of orientation as to time, place, and person soon become evident. One patient may become lost in the street, another may mistake a strange child for a relative, a third may have forgotten that his much loved wife is dead, and a fourth may give a large sum of money to a servant girl believing the latter to be a daughter. Such patients are often victimized by swindlers.

Pedantry, crass egoism, pathological suspiciousness, and sordid avarice may be met with among senile dements. The patients show absence of mental clarity, and episodes of clouding of consciousness and so-called twilight states are common. Senile dementia and "second childhood" were well depicted by Shakespeare in King Lear, who did not know where he had lodged the night before, nor whence the garments that he wore had come; "the foolish, fond old man, fourscore and upward," had become a babe again.

Pathological irritability is frequently observed, but the abnormal emotion, even when it is violent, usually subsides quickly. Disturbances in ethical domains (even sexual misdemeanors) are often attributable to limitations of associations, for when the bearing of the wrong behavior is explained to the senile dement, he may sometimes manifest normal repentance. Hallucinations (auditory more often than visual) and outspoken delusions (usually persecutory or hypochondriacal) may become manifest in later stages of the disease.

As the dementia advances, the behavior may become ever more foolish. An absurd will may be made, property may be sold for an amount far below what it is worth, or a silly marriage may be entered into. It is obvious that to prevent such unfortunate occurrences the existence of the senile dementia should be timely recognized so that the patients and their families may be adequately protected by transfer to suitable nursing homes or to psychiatric institutions, for custodial and palliative care.

Though the course of senile dementia is progressive, life may continue for many years, death ultimately occurring from some intercurrent disease like bronchopneumonia. Great care must be exercised to prevent senile dements (indeed all old people) from certain special injuries; thus many of them fracture the neck of the femur through slipping on a rug or in a bathtub.

Physicians have long been inclined to look upon mental diseases as being due to disorders of the brain and have hoped that through anatomical-histological, chemical, and physiological studies they might ultimately explain them. Such studies should certainly be diligently prosecuted; but psychiatry must also study human beings as wholes and take due account of instinctive urges, emotional experiences, interpersonal relationships, occupational settings, and economic and social conditions.

COMMENTS UPON THE CARE OF THE AGED

Man is an animal endowed with a truly marvelous group of harmonious complex regulatory functions; these have made it possible for him to remain relatively independent of his external environment despite the constantly changing influences of the external world. And in addition to the regulatory mechanisms inherent in his constitution, man now has the advantage of knowledge (thanks to modern civilization, science, and technique) that permits him to accommodate his needs systematically to varying conditions in order to avoid maladaptations.

But as life advances, the perfection of action of the inherent regulatory functions diminishes; people become more susceptible to heat and cold, their capacity to work and to sleep at high altitudes becomes less, the capacity of the circulatory system to adapt itself grows less perfect as shown by shortness of breath on exertion, the febrile reactions during infections are less marked than in youth, the thorax becomes more rigid as life advances and chronic bronchitis is common. The mortality rate of certain diseases (especially cardiovascular and infectious) increases by from 5 to 11 percent yearly when people are attacked by them after the age of thirty.

Our knowledge of the slow decline of the functions of man's organs and of his various faculties would seem to teach us that activities in their entirety should be very gradually adapted to this decline, since abrupt and profound changes in the mode of life of a man are likely to be harmful. At middle age, all sensible people should think of what later life may have in store for them and should begin gradually to make the adaptations that are desirable, rather than postpone them to a period when the changes will have to be made rapidly rather than by degrees.

The decline of the various capacities of man is in the main determined by the germ plasm from which he starts, rather than by the so-called "wear and tear" of life. Studies of identical twins indicate that they are prone to develop almost identical pathological changes in later life even when they have lived under different external conditions, have followed different occupations, and have lived in different places. Vogt has made a report upon eighty-two year old identical twins that exhibited an extraordinary agreement in senile traits —white hair, baldness, wrinkling of face, beginning cataracts, and so forth. Vogt believes the germ plasm had determined the development of all these things eighty-two years earlier; they could not be ascribed to external influences.

The same writer tells of two men aged sixty-three (identical twins), one of whom had been an office worker, the other a farm worker of the peasant class. Both of these men developed a particular contracture which was formerly attributed to external factors; Vogt feels sure that the germ plasm was responsible—the fertilized ova dictated the development of the contractures. All modern study suggests the inevitability of the phenomena of old age; these vary as the germ plasm varies; but we can do little to prevent their development, though we can do much toward increasing the comfort and palliating the ills of the old.

The relative numbers of old people are rapidly increasing in the United States; it has been estimated that by 1975 there will be some 30 million persons over sixty and some 22 million over sixty-five years of age. Many of these will be indigent and will have to be cared for by private or public charity. Our government has made some attempt to provide "old age security" for those who are not gainfully employed, but only a beginning has been made. Moreover, the old need more than a little money; they need to feel that they can still be of use to society, that they are not "laid on the shelf."

Much harm has resulted from compulsory retirement of persons who have reached a certain age irrespective of the state of their physical and mental health, for this often makes them grow old rapidly and dangerously. Retirement should be discretionary rather than arbitrary at any definite chronological age; each individual case should be decided for itself on its own merits, for some men are more efficient at seventy-five than others are at fifty. The Baltimore and Ohio Railway some time ago refused to accept the resignation of its president, Daniel Willard, though he was seventy-nine years old.

However, if retirement of a person from his regular occupation for any reason becomes necessary, arrangements should be made to keep him engaged in other and possibly related activities of which he is still capable, to permit him to make use for the good of society of the skill he still possesses, for otherwise it might be difficult for him to maintain his morale and his feelings of independence and happiness.

HOUSING OF THE OLD

Old people who are relatively well should, whenever possible, live in their own homes or in the homes of relatives, for they will, as a rule, be far happier there than in "homes for the aged," though residence in the latter may be necessary for some old people for economic reasons.

Even the chronically ill old person may be better off in his own home under the care of his family physician than in any other place. When removal to a hospital, to a home for the chronically sick, or to a home for the aged becomes unavoidable, care should be taken to see to it that the institution chosen (whether it be public or private) is properly organized for its work. A recent laudable attempt to give adequate care to the aged sick is to be seen in the opening of the Welfare Hospital in New York City; it is entirely devoted to the treatment of the ailments of the aged and is well equipped for the work. How much can be done for the salvaging of aged persons by the use of a standardized technique has been shown by the psychologist, Lillien J. Martin, founder and until her recent death director of the Old Age Counselling Center in San Francisco.

CLIMATES FOR THE OLD

When the economic situation permits of it, old people, especially if they are feeble, will do well to spend their winters in the South and their summers in the North. When this is not feasible, precautions should be taken to arrange for adequate protection from cold on the one hand and excessive heat on the other. Special Southern villages for elderly people have recently been advocated, to be populated chiefly by men and women over sixty-five, living in houses built especially for their convenience, centrally heated and supplied with community kitchens.

NURSING OF OLDER PATIENTS

Modern nursing has learned how to be of great help and comfort to old persons who are chronically ill or markedly enfeebled. A good bed about two feet from the floor, with a comfortable mattress protected in the middle by a piece of rubber sheeting or oil cloth, is desirable.

Daily care of the skin and of the mouth and teeth is important. After the cleansing bath, an alcohol rub or rubbing mineral oil on the skin may be resorted to. Bedsores should be prevented by avoidance of too prolonged pressure upon any part through frequent change of position (every two or three hours day and night), by keeping the lower bedding free from wrinkles and from crumbs of food. If a red spot should appear, the attention of the physician should be called to it. To avoid the long continuance of a recumbent position which favors the development of hypostatic pneumonia, the older person should sit up in an easy chair occasionally, or use a back rest in the bed. If hot-water bags have to be used, the temperature should not exceed 120 degrees.

Food should be served on an attractive tray. The amount of water to be permitted will be decided by the physician.

It is part of the nurse's duty to endeavor to maintain a habit in the patient of regular evacuation of the bowels daily and to see that the bladder is emptied routinely. Purgatives can usually be avoided; in some cases mineral oil by mouth will be helpful; occasionally a cleansing enema may be necessary but the formation of an enema habit is undesirable.

Old people should take a nap after the midday meal. If they wake early in the morning, suitable reading matter should be at the bedside.

When insomnia is marked, a glass of hot milk at 10 P.M. may

promote sleep. Hypnotics like bromides and barbiturates are to be avoided as far as possible since old people often do not tolerate them well; many find that a little whisky* and water at bedtime acts better when a sedative is needed. There should be an electric lamp on the table at the patient's bedside, also a bell by which the nurse or some member of the family can be summoned.

When the patient is able to be up and about, some exercise should be encouraged—a short walk or a motor ride, or a little work in a garden. But the greatest care should be exercised to prevent accidents, especially fracture of the neck of the femur.

Patients who are confined to bed should have some means of occupation there. Men may enjoy reading or listening to the radio; women, in addition to these activities, may wish to knit, crochet, or embroider.

The mental attitude of the nurse is very important. Cheerfulness, encouraging remarks, and willingness to gratify even trivial desires of the patient should be maintained. The patients' interest in personal appearance should be kept up; men should shave regularly, keep their hair tidy, and if up and about should have their clothing frequently pressed and kept spotless; a woman should be regularly manicured, have a hair wave occasionally, and be encouraged to keep herself well groomed by telling her "how well she looks."

* *Editor's note:* A little poem entitled "Longevity and Liquor" will be enjoyed by most readers, though not as a contribution to Dr. Barker's scientific discussion, even if he himself relayed it to the Editor, who is solely responsible for its publication here:

"The horse and the mule live 30 years
And know nothing of wine and beers,
The cow drinks water by the ton
And at 18 is nearly done.
The dog at 15 cashes in
Without the aid of rum or gin.
The cat in milk and water soaks
And then at 12 short years it croaks.
The modest, sober, bone dry hen
Lays eggs for nogs, then dies at 10.
All animals are strictly dry,
They sinless live and swiftly die,
But sinful, ginful, rum-soaked men
Survive for three score years and ten.
And some of us, the mighty few,
Stay pickled till we're 92!"

Anon.

Thus in many ways the nurse can be of mental help to the patient, especially if she has a genuine liking for human beings and a normal capacity for friendliness.

DIET IN OLD AGE

Most older people have lost some weight in later life; old age is proverbially the time of "the lean and slippered pantaloon." But both obesity and undue emaciation are to be avoided; the weight should be kept preferably within ten pounds of the average weight for the person's height. It is better to be somewhat underweight in old age than to be overweight if one desires to have a long life.

Four or five small meals rather than three large ones will often be found to be advantageous, and the diet should contain adequate amounts of protein, carbohydrate, animal fats, mineral salts, vitamins, and water. In some parts of the country inadequate diets depend upon ignorance or upon adverse economic conditions; the marked anaemias among people of Puerto Rico, and the widespread incidence of pellagra in some of our Southern States are instances in point.

But most old people whose dietary intake is inadequate have abnormal fear of food or have defective appetites. Many of them have been told that they should avoid meats for fear of autointoxication; others have been warned against eating much in general in old age; still others choose their foods faultily because of loss of teeth. A few old people are allergic to certain foods and in restricting their diets go farther than necessary; I am myself allergic to mushrooms but I can still ingest an abundant diet while eschewing the soups or other foods that contain mushrooms.

One cannot have the energy normal to his age if he is neglectful of proper food-intake. Many become faddists about food because of the extravagant claims of charlatans, or because of advice given by well-meaning but over-apprehensive relatives who insist upon special diets.

If an all-round diet of meat, chicken, fish, milk, cereals containing bran, potatoes, whole-wheat bread and butter, green vegetables, fruits, simple desserts, and water be regularly taken, there should be no dietetic deficiency, provided of course that the processes of digestion and absorption are not too much impaired.

I would emphasize especially that such a diet contains plenty of all necessary vitamins and mineral salts. The public has been almost too greatly "vitamin conscious" in recent years, due in part to the spread of knowledge concerning the importance of vitamins, in part to the extravagant claims of the salesmen of especial vitamin preparations.

In old age, when vitamin deficiency is met with it is most often a deficiency of the vitamin B-complex or of vitamin C. But anyone who eats liver occasionally, takes milk and orange juice daily, and uses brown bread (instead of white), as well as bran flakes twice a week will get plenty of vitamins B and C.

When mastication is badly impaired, soft foods must be largely used, the meats being hashed, some of the vegetables passed through a colander, and the bread or toast softened in milk. The services of a good dentist may be needed to improve the masticatory powers.

Provided the groups of food stuffs I have referred to are adequately represented in the diet, the physician may be liberal as to the particular members of the groups that are selected by his patients. Indeed, it is desirable that the foods should be enjoyed and that each should within the limits imposed gratify the particular taste.

Personally, I have found the following diet satisfactory:

1) Glass of water on rising.
2) *Breakfast:* orange juice or grapefruit, cereal, egg and bacon (or occasionally fried liver), buttered toast, marmalade, glass of milk, and coffee with sugar and cream.
3) *Luncheon:* cold or hot meat or fish (once a week fried sausage with waffles and maple syrup), brown bread and butter, lettuce and tomato salad, stewed or raw fruit, demitasse of coffee.
4) *Afternoon:* tea with cake.
5) *Dinner:* soup, meat, fowl, or fish, potatoes, two green vegetables, dessert (pudding or fruit), Sanka.

I rarely take a second helping of anything and I eat just enough to keep my weight practically stationary at 176 pounds.*

ENDOCRINE DEFICIENCIES IN OLD AGE

Much has been written upon endocrine deficiencies in elderly people, but marked hormonal lack is less common than the literature would lead one to believe. It is true that hormone production like other functional activities suffers some decline in old age, but this as a rule is not great enough to give rise to symptoms.

On account of the changes that occur in the sexual life in senescence, it was hoped that the administration of sex hormones might prove to be of value. The injection of female sex hormones at the change of life in women does have some beneficial effect in combating menopausal symptoms (hot flushes, and so forth). Injections of male sex hormones have been used in old men, not for their aphrodisiac effects but in the hope that they might lessen benign prostatic obstruction, or increase vigor and the general feeling of well-being. Though benefits have been reported, they have been less striking than had been hoped for, since prostatic obstruction is not relieved (it may even be increased) and the improvement in general well-being in old men is far less spectacular than had been expected by many.

SURGERY IN OLD AGE

It is amazing to find how well the aged tolerate even major surgery despite the decline of their general powers of resistance. With suitable preoperative preparation and postoperative care, cautious anaesthesia, and skillful surgical technique the mortality from surgery in the old has grown ever less. Removal of the pros-

* *Editor's Note:* A humorous commentary on Dr. Barker's remarks on diet is to be found in the following bit of verse—

"Here's to Methuselah—
Who ate all that he found on his plate
With no thoughts or worries as to amounts of calories
Or of his desserts' lack of animal fats or proteins
He had no food fancies or fears.
And yet he lived over 900 years!"

Anon.

tate, resection of the stomach, hysterectomy, and operations for removal of cancer and for strangulated hernia—all these surgical procedures have been safely carried out in people over seventy. One woman 106 years old was successfully operated upon for strangulated femoral hernia, and a 110 year-old colored man underwent a prostatectomy in 1939 and was alive and well a year later! Fractures of the neck of the femur, common in the old, are now overcome by fixation by means of the flanged nail under spinal anaesthesia; splints and casts are no longer necessary, and the patient may be kept in a wheel chair rather than in bed after the operation.

MENTAL HYGIENE AND PSYCHOTHERAPY FOR OLDER PERSONS

In old age, there is often exacerbation of earlier tendencies to anxiety, irritability, moodiness, egocentricity, sensitiveness, and suspicion. The general impairment of faculties in the old often makes them fearful, relatively hopeless, bewildered, and depressed. As their friends and relatives die off, they become more and more isolated, feel lonely, and are prone to develop hypochondriacal and sometimes paranoid ideas; it is but little wonder that suicide is not uncommon among the aged.

Mental rigidity and a tendency to rut formation tend to increase with the advancing years. The problems have been ably discussed by the psychologist Dr. George Lawton. In my own little book *Psychotherapy* (1940), I have emphasized the importance of gradual diminution of the demands made upon the mind and body of persons over sixty. Hours of work should be lessened and time devoted to rest and recreation should be correspondingly increased. Exercise should be regularly taken but it should be gentle, never violent. Bodily and mental fatigue should be sedulously avoided. Men engaged in business or professional life should gradually delegate more and more responsibility to their associates, reserving their own powers for the more important duties and decisions and for the giving of wise counsel to their juniors.

Should the time for retirement come, social, altruistic, or literary interests may be resorted to as substitutes for former activities. Some may find pleasure in writing their autobiographies; a veritable flood of these has recently been in evidence. Others who enjoy travel may visit distant countries or even make a trip around the world. The wise family physician will know how to give the advice most suitable to the individual case.

The psychotherapeutic measures that are most serviceable for old persons include suggestion, persuasion, and guidance as to the readjustment of hopes and ambitions. Also valuable is the development of a sane philosophy with willingness to face reality as it has become, accepting with stoicism increasing limitations without striving for what is no longer possible.

Though Freud thought that psychoanalysis was scarcely applicable in old age, owing to loss of personal elasticity and the long experience of the old person that would have to be investigated, we must gratefully admit that the psychoanalytic method has shown itself to be a valuable instrument of research for giving us a better understanding of the personality changes, the libidinous rearrangements and the regressions that occur late in life.

PESSIMISM OR OPTIMISM REGARDING OLD AGE

From the earliest times, both medical and lay writers have differed much in their estimation of the desirability of old age. The viewpoint of many has been gloomy; others have emphasized the brighter side. There can be no question that in pathological old age the debit side of the ledger greatly exceeds the credit side; such longevity cannot be considered desirable. Physiological old age is a different matter, though some assume that even in it the balance sheet is still heavily overweighted in the debit direction.

Anthony Trollope in his novel *The Fixed Period* suggested the desirability of putting persons painlessly to death when they approached the age of seventy. The political economist and humorist Stephen Leacock thinks that "the only good thing you can say about old age is that it is better than being dead"; it is the "Front Line" of life, moving into "No Man's Land," which is covered with mist, and in it one has an increasing feeling of isolation, though there is some consolation if one has something to pass on—the new life of children and of grandchildren, or if not that, at least some recollection of good deeds, or of something done that may give one the hope of being able to say "non omnis moriar" (I shall not altogether die). He concludes his article (published in the *New York Times Magazine* on the day after he became seventy) by exclaiming: "Give me my stick. I'm going out on to No Man's Land. I'll face it."

The late Sir William Osler at the age of fifty-six, under the emotional strain of leaving America and saying farewell to his friends here, seemed pessimistic when he spoke of the "relative uselessness of persons over sixty." Sir William however, lived to be over seventy and exerted a profound influence upon medicine and upon the general public during the last fourteen years of his life.

Dr. A. S. Warthin of Ann Arbor thought that old age should be met with courage; he emphasized especially the many compensations of the seventh and eighth decades of life due to the fact that spiritual and mental functions are preserved longer than others. But he counted the old person fortunate, even though still capable of intellectual pleasures, if he were blessed with a speedy release before the unhappy days of second childhood came upon him.

The athlete and sculptor R. Tait McKenzie looked upon old age favorably for its gain in physical and mental poise, for its accumulated experience and skills, for its knowledge of ways of saving mental and physical energy, for the satisfaction of doing well and easily things that younger men would have to struggle over unsuccessfully. He valued his contacts with fine minds and personalities, and his better understanding of fine literature. The physical losses of age were balanced by flattering recollections of the fine animal he once had been, and the reduced ability for prolonged effort was compensated for by his reserves of knowledge and experience. With Audrey Brown he said "I shall grow old with autumn and not reluctantly," and in any case he felt it his duty to maintain his fortitude until the end.

The Swiss neurologist C. von Monakow, who lived to be seventy-seven, wrote during the last few months of his life a panegyric upon natural old age, maintaining that it was far less sad than pessimistic writers would have us believe. He could still make intellectual gains and experience further growth in mental values and capacities. He developed an increased interest in ultimate problems that gave wings to his thoughts and to his deeds. He even wrote a large monograph entitled *The Emotions, Mortality, and the Brain.* Though he suffered a decrease of satisfaction in bodily pleasures and a lessening of concern regarding his own personal survival, he found compensation in greater regard for the welfare and future of his offspring, of the nation, and of the whole of humanity.

Having myself reached the age of seventy-four, I can say that I have had the good fortune to have lived longer than the average. Because of long-lived Canadian ancestors and a relatively favorable environment, I also have escaped thus far most of the infirmities and disabilities that all too often accompany longevity.

I am reconciled to the fact that the duration of human life is definitely limited but shall be glad to continue to live as long as I can be professionally and socially useful, hoping however that when usefulness is over, release may come painlessly, and all the better if suddenly, without my being required to linger on for a long time as a burden to myself or to others.

I still have great pleasure in unraveling the tangled skeins of intricate and difficult medical diagnostic problems in hospitals and in private practice and in planning comprehensive therapeutic regimes suited to the management of multidimensional diagnostic findings.

As to ultimate philosophical considerations, I can truthfully say that I was more concerned with them in my youth than I have been during the approach to senescence. I am grateful for having been privileged to live during a marvelous period of medical and scientific advances. It has been a joy to watch, and to endeavor to participate in, the conquest of a large number of the infectious diseases and the extension of preventive sanitary measures, to witness the extraordinary progress of our knowledge of nutrition, metabolism, and endocrinology during the fifty years that have elapsed since I graduated in medicine, to learn how to make use of the newer physical, chemical, biological, and psychological technical methods, and to observe the beneficial effects of penetrating the bodies of sick human beings with the magic bullets of salvarsan, sulfanilamide, and sulfapyridine. Within a few hours, my chauffeur can bring me from the medical libraries of the city fifty books or articles in English, French, and German bearing upon any topic in which I am interested.

The telephone, electric lighting, the automobile, the airplane, the X-ray, radium, the moving picture, the radio, electrical refrigeration in homes, air conditioning, synthetic textiles, and television are all developments of the period through which I have lived. On flying to Oklahoma City and back recently, it seemed almost incredible that I could reach Chicago in less than four hours after leaving Washington and that I could be in Oklahoma City in six and a half hours after leaving Chicago. It continues to astound me that I can sit before my radio in the evening and within fifteen minutes hear four short talks about war conditions from London, Berlin, Paris, and Rome.*

I am daily thankful that it has been my lot to live in the United States of America rather than in a country that is under an iniquitous totalitarian government. I have greatly enjoyed reading *Gone with the Wind*, and have been deeply moved by the perusal of *Grapes of Wrath*, and a little later found it possible to see and hear the characters of both books in the moving pictures. Among my pet diversions are solving the crossword puzzles in the London *Daily Times*, wrestling each week-end with Elizabeth Kingsley's double acrostic in the *Saturday Review of Literature*, and participating in an occasional game of contract bridge.

Even to the bodily pleasures I am not wholly indifferent, for I

* [*Editor's Note:* This paper was written before the United States entered the war.]

enjoy a mild cigar after each meal, a glass or two of good wine at a dinner party, and the oysters, terrapin, soft-shelled crabs, and fried chicken of Maryland!

In addition to unusually happy marital and familial experiences, I have been blessed with loyal associates and a host of good friends and acquaintances who have added hugely to the joys of my life. With R. Tait McKenzie I must admit that I have "had a good run" and that I should be willing to "call it a day," and for my friends I can wish nothing better than that they may have as many happy memories as I have when they approach the sunset of their lives.*

* *Editor's Note:* The Editor was reading the proofs of this chapter when he learned of Dr. Barker's death on July 13, 1943, at the age of 76, and after one year's illness. Dr. Barker was indeed a fortunate man: to have lived so useful and noble a life and then to have crowned it with an old age which may stand for a beautiful symbol of what every old age should be!

APPLYING MENTAL HEALTH PRINCIPLES TO PROBLEMS OF THE AGING

By Nolan D. C. Lewis *

THE TERM "senile" seems descriptive of a rather simple situation: we have an old person, and that is the senile state! Really the matter is extremely complex.

The period of life known as the "senium," or "old age," is associated with many problems which are peculiar, distinct, and often quite remote in character from those encountered in infancy and the earlier adult years. Much of the knowledge gained from the study of the physical and mental behavior of young and middle-aged adults can no more be applied to the period of senility than to the immediate life of the child. Moreover, "age" is an extremely elastic term which, in physiological concepts, can rarely be used in its chronological sense, as what is understood by "age" in terms of structure-function may overtake a man in his earlier years or may manifest itself in irregular retardations and dysfunctions of special sets of organs, according to the results of predisposition, previous diseases, and the stress and wear and tear to which the body has been subjected in its journey through life.

In a manner of speaking, some individuals are old and worn-out in childhood. There are many old people who are old in years and yet are quite useful. As we grow older we are inclined to use the term senility to describe people who are a little ahead of us in years. When we were children, we thought those a few years ahead of us in age were "old." We must take into consideration many different kinds of ages: mental, moral, physiological, and chronological. The following story is a good illustration of the possible variety of ages.

* Director, New York State Psychiatric Institute and Hospital, New York City.

"An old Boston gentleman, wishing to be friendly toward a little boy, asked him, 'And how old are you, son?' The boy answered at length, 'If you are asking how old I am mentally, according to intelligence tests, I am 12 years old. Morally I am 5 years of age, and physically I am ten years of age, but I assume you are referring to that old term, chronological age. If you are, I am eight years old.' "

In senility, we deal with biological as well as chronological age, since age is a matter of biology as well as chronology. In the individual, from the time he is conceived and on through maturity, there are going on at the same time degenerative or involutionary processes of the tissues as well as growth. Senility, therefore, starts with conception.

Each individual is born with certain endowments or capacities and with the ability to mature. These capacities are unequal in strength and function, there being many degrees of power, and it should be recognized that a number of them grow progressively weaker after the individual has passed the prime of life. These irregularities in capacity account for many, if not most, of the individual differences in attitude and behavior.

Development of the organs goes on at irregular speeds throughout life. Post-mortems on all sorts of people show that even in the very aged there are always a few organs that are relatively young. Some organs do not show the advance of age; some grow old faster than others. Biological time rather than chronological time is important. For some reason, human beings do not live more than 100 years, and this is probably a good thing. If we lived to be 1,000 years old we would have ten times as many accidents and diseases, and our bodies would have to function at a very low level.

In old age, whether chronological or physiological, some important endowments and functions have attenuated, have become distorted through conversion, or have disappeared entirely. Thus we are dealing with a different individual after age has required the readjustment of the whole psychobiological reaction setting.

For some reason, scientific study of the old person has been neglected; there have been frequent studies of childhood but hardly any of old age. As compared with the interest taken in children's problems by general physicians, psychiatrists, psychologists, social workers, and public-welfare organizations, the interest and care accorded the aged is insignificant, amounting to nothing less than neglect. Here and there one finds a small organization interested in old people, but chiefly from the standpoint of housing and feeding—in other words, with an eye to economic welfare. There is an enormous field here for research. But where do we find journals devoted to the welfare of the aged? One may admit some excuse for this attitude on the basis that the aged are generally, although by no means always, economically worthless, and become more so with added years, while the child has an increasing economic value and, in addition, a prospective maturity which may be favorably influenced by helpful interference at the proper maturation phases. Perhaps, too, doctors have not made a specialty of geriatrics, and investigators have side-stepped the field because of a subtle unconscious fear of getting old themselves.

Inasmuch as one person's tissues may become senile long before another's and reveal what is known as senility in degrees which vary from those manifested by other individuals, we must expect to find and we do find varying degrees of functional loss and distortion. Categorically, we refer to the span of life after the sixtieth year as the senile period, and our remarks in general refer to this period, although they apply as well to exceptional cases in the younger age periods. (Some elements in the senile deterioration begin at birth or even before, and usually at forty-eight or fifty years the changes characteristic of senility become evident in the human organism.)

Senility is simply one aspect of the developmental process. The gradual change from the adult state to old age is essentially a normal biologic reaction characterized by certain physiologic alterations which in themselves complicate and disturb the life adjustments. Moreover, like all other processes in the living organism, these changes are often accentuated or distorted by pathologic variations. In every instance, there is some degree of senile atrophy of cells, tissues, organs, and organ systems, and in a complex organism like man, different cells and tissues grow old at different rates of speed. That both men and animals gradually age—that is, become senile in the course of progressive development—is indicated by the decrease in the metabolic rate.

In senility the condition of the blood vessels is important. Some thickening takes place, and there may be a predisposition to this. Although our knowledge is yet far from complete as to vascular and endocrine changes that contribute to or are associated with senility, it is certain that there is normally a decrease in the elasticity and contractibility of the blood vessels, which may be so excessive as to constitute pathologic arteriosclerosis, and which in any case throws an increased load upon the heart and interferes as well with the general nutrition of the body. Some show it in the brain and not in other organs, and we find all sorts of combinations. *Senility and arteriosclerosis are not synonymous terms.* An old person with a mental disease may or may not have arteriosclerosis; some types of mental disorder may occur in the old person where there is no arteriosclerosis. As he grows older, a person functions a little less actively, and we find at the end these so-called changes of senility. By post-mortem examination of an individual's brain, we can tell whether or not it is that of an old person, but we cannot tell whether he was a so-called normal person or one who had been severely ill mentally.

One might discuss the nature of the process of senescence in the light of a number of hypotheses. However, opinions on the subject may be divided in a general way into two main groups: one considers senescence as a multicellular phenomenon, while the other regards it as an inherent property of the individual cells. The irregularities noted in the senile developments in the various organs and parts of the body would favor the latter point of view.

It may be said that the longevity of the cell varies inversely as the rate of energy expended in metabolism, and the fundamentals of longevity are sought among the factors of heredity, sex, race, and mode of life. It has been pointed out that the basal metabolism of people above the age of fifty years is lower than that of younger people, and that the decrease is brought about gradually without a sudden drop in any particular age group; the rate of decrease is about 3 to 5 percent in each ten-year period.

Along with the diminution in physical strength and activity there appears a depressive mental attitude, probably due to the recognition or the anticipation of the approach of old age, with its unfulfilled hopes and plans, and the increasing difficulty in dealing with the ordinary problems of life—a failure of compensation at the psychological level where conflicts, formerly resolved successfully, now break through and overwhelm such constructive forces as are available. The failure of the psychological protective processes may be enhanced by, or associated with, the vascular changes of senility, as well as with other complicating physical and toxic factors.

Among the universally recognized features of senility, the effects of which should be combatted by all the means at the disposal of physicians and others, are the impairment of retentive ability and the general failure of memory, and depression, fears, and self-depreciation, with loss of confidence in ability, all of which may be increased or brought into prominence by overwork or fatigue in complicated situations which were once handled with ease, but which now, because of increased fatigability, become almost impossible burdens. Many are able to work steadily and comfortably without difficulty, but at a much lower mental level than the original one attained with ease; and as the old person is struggling to keep his place in the world, the hygienist should weigh all factors carefully before interfering with any work program. The "puttering" activities of the aged, so frequently called "imaginary duties" by relatives and associates who are annoyed by what appears to be unimportant work or actual obstructions to the work of others, are of the utmost psychobiological importance to the individual, as they are saving mechanisms by which he holds on to his ego importance in the world.

There are as many differences of character and reactions among the aged as among developing children. We find degrees of irritability (especially at night), fear responses, reactive depressions, addiction to routine, dissatisfaction with the work and lives of others, and mild, but often justified, ideas of persecution. The basis of this last is the lack of sympathy and understanding shown to the emotional life and needs of the aged.

Many old people become sad, disillusioned, and disappointed, and life often is empty and miserable as they grow more or less incapable of playing useful roles in the family circle. However, they are not infrequently prevented from making themselves useful by impatient relatives who neglect to make the necessary special arrangements to aid the adjustment or who fail to give any special attention to the problem. The old are too often regarded as a heavy burden upon the finances and emotions of the family group, and as a result they become the objects either of open antagonism or of suppressed and subtle ill-will. Old age pensions are relieving many such family situations.

Many persons find little if any difficulty in making the adjustments incident and necessary to old age. Others are reluctant to relinquish the activities formerly pursued, wish to continue their work and their pleasures as formerly, and, in spite of an obviously failing capacity, become charged with the belief that they are as good as ever. When pressure is brought to bear upon one of these situations, a great deal of tact is necessary, inasmuch as a pathological response may be easily effected. The older person may look upon a particular change as evidence of a tragic loss in his life, such realization may precipitate a psychotic episode of some severity, and this last will still further complicate the powers of adjustment.

"The subject of old age has never been a popular one with the medical profession." * There are more reasons for this than the one usually offered—the lack of economic importance of the old person in our society. Although there are plenty of exceptions, old people are not as a rule pleasant patients, and moreover the conditions and types of disease from which they suffer are apt to be therapeutically hopeless or at best to lend themselves only to symptomatic relief. It may be also said that the aged are unpleasant, even repulsive, from the aesthetic standpoint, the degree being determined both by the condition of the patient and by the aesthetic state and capacities of

* M. Critchley, "The Neurology of Old Age," *Lancet*, CCXX (May 23, 1931), 1119.

the observer. They are sufficiently repelling to counteract the sympathetic feelings and tendencies of those inclined by nature to respond to helplessness, personal difficulties, and illness in others. "We can readily account for the public neglect of the aged. Human sympathy is universal in its scope, but not in its application. Instinctively or subconsciously, economic value, social relations, the aesthetic sense, and other factors influence the directions in which sympathy is applied. . . . Optimistic philosophers of all ages from Cicero to Jean Finot describe old age as being beautiful, but no philosopher has ever declared that the aged themselves were beautiful." *

There are several physical and mental characteristics of old persons which, with exceptions, account for their unpleasantness or repulsiveness to others. Of the former, there are the various evidences of physical decay and distortion, which carry with them implications threatening the future; disagreeable odors and frequently neglect of clothing and other duties of cleanliness and personal hygiene. The mental reasons are probably by far the more important, and the behavior of the senile is frequently annoying, displaying peevishness, irritability, willfulness, childishness, ill-tempered and offensive behavior, expressions of depressed feelings, foolish obsessions and suspicions, and a tendency to prolixity and to prolonged conversations in which past experiences are related without discrimination as to what is important and what irrelevant. The aged are usually selfish, or at least their attitudes and reactions in special situations are so interpreted. Many suffer from ill-health, over which they become worried and depressed, some to such an extent that suicide is selected as a way out. Some combination of these expressions is present in practically every aged individual, and if it is not neutralized by an understanding attitude on the part of companions, it will act destructively and counteract sympathy and active interest in the welfare of the old.

There are logical reasons for the unpleasant mental attitude of the aged person. The energy, capacity, and enthusiasm of youth are gone, and with them a certain degree of the ability to adjust to the complex and ever-changing circumstances of life. As a result,

* M. W. Thewlis, *Geriatrics*. St. Louis, C. V. Mosby Co., 1919 ed.

in the midst of the decline in life, their attitude can be none too optimistic, and it is not strange that any unusual occurrence in the family routine, any increased pressure of extraneous circumstances, stressful situations, or unexpected disappointments, may partially or even totally overwhelm them.

The retained constitutional capacity for adaptation may in large part determine whether the reaction released will be merely an exaggeration of the usual senile tendency to ruminate over losses, a domination by self-centered ideas or regretful thoughts and doubts of the present, or feelings of inadequacy, weariness, and resignation toward the future. When the make-up is more rigid, rendering adaptability still more difficult, there will be more serious responses, with depression in pure form, or with agitation and self-depreciation, accompanied by pronounced disorders of sleep and digestion. Fluctuating mental confusion, apathetic states, and episodes of elation resembling a manic reaction, with exaggerated ideas of self-importance, are occasionally released in similar circumstances.

In some seniles there is a phase of behavior which is known as "sexual recrudescence." This may express itself in the form of foolish infatuations for younger persons of the opposite sex, revealing itself in talk and silly actions noticeable only to the immediate family or to the interested neighbors, or its expression may become a source of active annoyance to the household servants, to others outside the home, or to acquaintances living at distances who may be selected as love objects. The activity may be diffuse or sharply localized to one love object. It may lead to medico-legal action, and in the case of old men with latent or revived character twists or with psychoses, it may result in the seduction or rape of young children or of mature women. This same trend or drive may lead to marriages displeasing to relatives because of inheritance or other rights. It must be remembered that the old person sometimes is hypersuggestible and rather susceptible to the possibilities of friendship, whatever the source. These marriages or threatened marriages may become the foci of many unhappy affairs, while the immediate participants may be discontented or happy in their intimate personal relationship.

In women, in addition to the possibility of an erotic flair in senility, the maternal instinct—or whatever it is that is usually known as the "maternal instinct"—may be markedly in evidence. This is true even of aged virgins, and the tendency may survive even after the higher intellectual faculties have disappeared, as is amply demonstrated daily on the wards of large institutions for the mentally ill, where aged women habitually play with dolls or become attached to feebleminded and often partially helpless children for whom they show genuine maternal solicitude, including feeding, personal hygiene, caressing, and attention to general welfare and protection. Such a self-appointed "mother" often becomes seriously disturbed and unhappy if the child dies or is otherwise removed. The persistence of this motherly attitude is to be noted not only in institutional seniles, but also in the normal ones at home, where their need for love and their craving for attention create family difficulties, particularly in the grandchildren situation. The possible grandparent-child-parent relationships, hates, loves, jealousies, conflicts, and complications are too well known to elaborate here.

Why some seniles show merely a quantitative decrease in abilities, capacities, and adaptations, while others exhibit pathological deviations and finally develop active mental disorder, is an unsolved problem which emphasizes the need of studying the physiologic and psychologic aspects of old age with more precision. So far, investigations of the physical factors have not only failed to reveal important differences, but similarities have been found in the brains of cases of senile dementia and of normal seniles. Moreover, there is a lack of correlation between the severity of the pathological changes and the degree of intellectual impairment, and equally severe alterations have been found in the brains of old persons of normal mentality.

Everywhere the usual personal problems will arise and must be met by the individual. If there is an incapacity to adjust to the more serious personal problems, these situations may precipitate a senile psychosis. If there is sufficient unimpaired compensatory ability in the integration, the adjustment may occur without the development of a psychosis. There is a wide range of difference between individuals in their capacities to compensate for untoward environmental factors as well as for the numerous lesions in the body, including the brain. A lesion in the brain, a toxic focus in the body, or a thwarting family situation may release a psychosis in one individual, while another individual may bring into play compensatory capacities and adjustments and show no evidence of a psychosis.

With respect to psychoses, I should like to point out that when an old person is brought into the hospital with a mental disorder, if he is sixty years or older, his case is put into the category of senile psychosis, provided the individual has not had periods of mental trouble earlier in his life. If it is not just another attack, and the person is not merely repeating something he had had previously but becomes mentally ill for the first time, we feel that the aging process has had something to do with his breaking down.

The term "senile disorder" is a wide generalization. There is only one thing about which we can generalize, and that is in all senile psychoses there are three cardinal symptoms. Other symptoms and other changes serve to further differentiate them.

1. Disturbance of the memory. These are exaggerations of memory limitations which we find in the normal old person.

2. Disturbance in judgment. In senile psychoses, the emotions throw adjustments out of gear and fine points cannot be decided.

3. The change in character itself. Originally we are all a specific type of personality. We are built according to the four types which describe people pretty well and which are to be recognized in the normal states of ordinary people. Each older person is already disposed toward a particular type of mental disorder, the same type he would have shown twenty years previously; the mental disorder is due to the whole personality, and when that breaks we bring into fruition all the difficulties of our lives. Hence, an equally important part of the phrase "aged personality" is "personality," and for that reason we should consider its chief types.

The first is the *schizoid*—the type that tends to splitting of the psyche. This characterizes shy, retiring personalities who are careful, deep thinkers. When these persons break down, they get definitely out of touch with the world and have feelings of unreality and splitting of the mind. Some precipitating factor may cause an old person who all his life has had a schizoid personality to break down; he then shows all the symptoms of splitting that a young person would show, *plus* the three cardinal symptoms already listed as characterizing the senile psychosis. The schizoid type becomes senile dementia; he just sits and doesn't do much else.

The second main type of personality is the *cycloid*, which is characterized by mood swings. This is the type of individual who is either "up" or "down"; he goes into the blues, and again is happy. Such an individual is more of the extrovert, a good executive type. When he is "high," he will push a big enterprise and succeed in it. An example is the scientist who at seventy years of age did not have a senile psychosis, but had had a depressed spell every ten years. The depression is due to old age only when the old person who comes to us has not previously had deep depressive spells.

The third type is the *paranoid*. These are very superior people even when they are old. They do not lose so much of their memories, and they may be quite difficult to get along with. They are a little more saucy, crotchety, and show a little less character change. These character patterns have always been strong. When they go into a mental disorder, they have delusions; they reason logically from false premises. They tell realistic and carefully constructed stories that are difficult to disprove. The paranoid says "something is so," his wife says "it is not so," but the neighbors say "it is a little bit so."

The last personality type is the *neurotic* individual who may or may not eventually develop a full-blown neurosis. The neurotic personality type shows a great lack of confidence and is extremely cautious, but can use his anxieties constructively and often gets along quite well.

One's personality is built from childhood; when a person breaks down, he breaks down along one of these four lines. The only new things in old age are the presence of the three cardinal symptoms of "senile disorder," which complicate the breakdown a little bit.

While mixtures are possible, a person is primarily one type or can be considered one, after you know him pretty well. There is no such thing as a normal person. Statistical or mathematical norms can be found, but in something like personality, which is dynamic and changing, we cannot measure exactly. All of us must travel within certain limits, or curbs; the mores or laws of society on the one hand, and our consciences on the other hand.

Senility is a period of life, like infancy and adulthood. After middle maturity, a division of adulthood, we come to late maturity, a period called senility. Properly used, it is a biological term, an aging process, a chronological distinction and should never be used to describe a disease of the mind or abnormal people. Senile psychosis should be used to describe mental disorders occurring in senility. An individual has a senile psychosis if he becomes mentally ill for the first time after he is sixty years of age.

A senile psychotic is less treatable than a more youthful one. Psychoses follow a general law of all chronic diseases, to wit, the longer the disease has existed, the less one can expect of treatment. Psychiatrists are no different from the surgeon who doesn't like to take a case if the appendix has burst, or the physician presented with a case of pneumonia that is very far advanced.

People come to psychiatric institutions after they are very sick. Today, we know that certain kinds of pains require attention by doctors; we should learn that certain ways of behaving are signs of mental and emotional illness and warrant treatment by a psychiatrist.

I should like to consider now the mental hygiene aspects of the old age problem. Hard-and-fast rules for avoiding or relieving troubles cannot be formulated (except not to abuse the patient.) Each individual is an entity in himself and each case is a problem for special study and recommendations. However, certain general considerations may be kept in mind by those who have responsibility for the aged. As examples of opportunities for helpful attitudes on the part of staffs in old age homes, social workers, physicians, etc., one might point out the following:

1. We must arrange to use the senile individual in an economic way, or at least in a fashion to assure him (or her) that he is still a part of the world of affairs. No one wants to be told he is on the shelf and no longer part of society.

2. Many facts indicate that a reasonable variety in mental occupation is a factor in retarding mental senility. What we often call mental fatigue may be something far less transitory than fatigue in the ordinary physical sense, and seniles fatigue easily and restitution is slow. Therefore, changes of work and frequent rest periods should be arranged. The old person feels fatigue a little sooner, but with shortened periods of labor he can do just as well as he ever did. He is not quite so adaptable or flexible, but this is a good thing from the standpoint of longevity. To live longer, one should not make much change in his physical habits. We should eat the same food, take the same exercise, get the same hours of sleep. But we also should change our mind and change our ideas a lot, taking up new interests before we get too old.

We ought to do as much work as possible in studying individual cases to see what stirs creative interests in one person and not in another. What must we play on in a particular person to get a particular response? Some people say there is no use in trying to change things after one is fifty years old. This is not so. All traits can be built up by habit. It takes only just a little bit longer for an old person to learn to do things. Six hours may be required to learn in old age what could be learned in five hours at age twenty-five, but still the older person can learn more easily at sixty-five than he could when he was twelve. It is true that confidence alone does not bring success. But without it, we cannot do anything. If you have no faith, you are licked.

Man is made for action, reproduction, creative work. As we get old, we do not do so much original work, but we still have the possibility of creating on a different level, the ego level.

3. If we want to deal honestly and well with the senile individual, we should relieve him as far as possible from worry, mental strain, anxieties, and feelings of financial insecurity. The old person should have a job to do, but we also should periodically withdraw him from the whirl of effortful existence. Some older persons enjoy spending longer periods of time under simple, pleasant conditions in retirement, away from annoyances, out of the influence of the

perpetual sense of hurry and the sequence of incidents which exhaust the attention and which are nowadays a part of practically every environment.

4. With the gradually devitalizing processes in mind, especial care should be taken to avoid physical discomforts, vitiated air, and overeating. Many elderly people eat too much and are unwise in their selection of foods. It is often astounding to note the relief from sluggishness, constipation, and irritability that can be obtained by making certain sensible modifications in the diets of older people and by giving attention to their elimination processes. The old person should be protected from infection; he is quite susceptible to pneumonia.

5. The senile should be protected from injuries, as he readily develops the post-traumatic constitution, with its characteristic changes in disposition. A physical trauma may definitely change the personality either temporarily or permanently or it may merely increase the general irritability which often becomes prominent in old people, particularly at night and early in the morning. Physical injuries may produce or increase a tendency to hypochondriasis and self-scrutiny, in addition to increasing the feeling of uncertainty that is already present.

6. It is important to avoid any heavy burden on the sense organs. Exhaustion of sight and hearing often seriously impairs social efficiency in the contacts made by senile individuals and helps to explain some of the personality changes. Tolerance of the situation and some aid from others may prevent a narrowing of the sphere of interests and a tendency to focus attention on the self.

7. The younger and more able associates of the senile should recognize and make allowances for his occasional loss of acuity in dealing with situations that require fine discrimination and tact, situations which in his earlier days he was able to handle perfectly. A little diplomacy and encouragement may do much to relieve the older individual's tension. In many disagreeable seniles, the picture is merely an exaggeration of an originally somewhat difficult personality of the projective type, in which self-control is now lost or weakened, allowing the character traits free play.

8. Tolerance and understanding should be exercised in connection with those aged people who by virtue of a temperament that may become exaggerated or distorted by complicating factors show a marked egoism, along with uneasiness, restlessness, and a tendency to harp on their difficulties. Some show a pronounced vulnerability of the psyche to small or relatively insignificant misunderstandings, which they may interpret as insults that provoke aggressive responses; while others react with a feeling of panic and complete helplessness whenever complicated situations present themselves. Thus the practical handling of these problems may be complicated in various ways, and requires some special study.

9. Finally, in a mental hygiene program for older people, we should give the aged individual some understanding of his personality in terms of the psychology of old age.

One cannot emphasize too strongly that chronological age is not an index of physiological age, or degree of deterioration. Therefore, each individual senile reaction must be considered in relation to the particular situation to be evaluated. But most cases should be approached with a realization that the physiological and mental mechanisms are less elastic than formerly, so that adjustments and compensations may not be readily accomplished.

There is unevenness in the emotions and in physiological make-up just as there is in muscular coördination. Jealous attitudes and sleeping difficulties may go along with deterioration of skills, neglect of the person, clothing, etc. These are typical of old people and must be taken into consideration when dealing with them.

To sum up, old people cannot all be treated alike: the old person does not lose his definite personality just because he is old. Moreover, the senile wants a job, wants to be important, wants affection and lots of it, and when he is denied importance, affection, and understanding, he becomes a problem. He certainly does not want people standing around in *bas relief*, waiting for him to die. The application of sound common sense, mixed with an understanding of the problems faced by the aged and reinforced by human sympathy, does much to smooth out the difficulties inherent in the nature of human relationships.

WORK THERAPY, INTERESTS, AND ACTIVITIES

By Edward Hochhauser *

In San Francisco several years ago I visited a home for the aged. I found a very happy group with a fine relationship existing between the superintendent and the residents. In discussing the interests and activities of the members and what part these played in their adjustment, the superintendent told of a man who at first made no friends and was disagreeable to the other guests as well as the staff. Attempts to interest him in work or activities of the institution failed, but before making a report to the board which would mean his discharge, the superintendent decided to try once more. Yes, there was one thing he would like to do. Ever since he was a young man he had wanted to raise cucumbers, but he knew this was impossible in a city institution with lawns and flower beds. He was told he could have his cucumber bed, and the next day a small plot was prepared. As the plants grew and blossomed he too blossomed into a friendly and even happy individual.

A new gardener had been engaged about this time; he had come well recommended. One morning a very distraught old man waited on the superintendent and reported that his cucumbers had been pulled up. The gardener was called in and admitted that he had pulled up the cucumbers, over the old man's protest, because they destroyed the appearance of the lawn. The superintendent advised him to find himself a new job, for if he could not understand what these cucumbers meant to this old man, he never could understand their institution.

Occupational therapy may be defined as mental or physical

* Executive Director, Committee for the Care of the Jewish Tuberculous, Inc., New York City.

activity definitely prescribed and guided for the specific purpose of hastening the recovery from the effects of disease or injury. If we add work therapy to this and include the aged as well as the handicapped we might consider the aim of such an approach to be the better adjustment of the individual to his fellows and to the limitations that his handicap places upon him. Work therapy under wise and skillful supervision gives purpose, responsibility, and satisfaction to physical activity, aiding in the readjustment of the aged and the rehabilitation of the physically and the mentally handicapped.

However, work therapy for the aged and for such a handicapped group as the tuberculous will have obvious differences in objectives and in procedures. With some of the tuberculous, the purpose is the return to normal life in industry and society. With others, who because of extensive disease require permanent sheltered employment, work therapy seeks to retain a maximum of health and satisfaction and provides an opportunity to make as large a contribution as is possible to their own economic status.

Work therapy for the aged has much in common with the permanent sheltered group who do not expect to return to industry. We cannot expect that work therapy for this group will be self-sustaining when measured by the report of a certified public accountant. We show a decided profit when we balance the financial results over against the social gains and consider the mental and physical well-being of the patient and those with whom he lives, the years of usefulness and satisfaction which are the consequence of work paid for and well done. With the aged or the handicapped who live in an institution and have unlimited time on their hands and nothing to do, institutional problems are complicated by ill-adjusted residents. Hence, the great value of purposeful and socially recognized activity.

Dr. Alexis Carrel in his *Man the Unknown* says "the aging man should neither stop working nor retire. Inaction further impoverishes the content of time. Leisure is even more dangerous for the old than for the young. To those whose forces are declining appropriate work should be given. But not rest."

Administrators and board members have the problem of administering their institutions as economically as possible. There are some institutions for the tuberculous that consider occupational therapy a luxury they believe they cannot afford. They believe that their only responsibility is to provide good food and medical care. Yet an increasing number of such institutions not only provide occupational therapy, but are adding educational courses that are cultural or recreational, as well as prevocational, and they justify the additional expense on the basis that they are doing a better job in getting the patients well and in aiding them to stay well.

We are basing our plea that work therapy be provided for the permanently sheltered type of patient on the ground that without it he is being prematurely condemned to the scrap heap. At what age may we be so consigned? I suspect that our answer will be colored by the age we happen to be.

Dr. Lillien J. Martin wrote: "What we have come to believe as a result of rehabilitation work with the old is that these people are just as subject to change and growth as in any other period of life, allowing always more time to effect the change in old age than in youth or childhood."

Can we say that time spent without satisfaction to oneself or to another is time misspent in youth but well spent in old age? At old age have we outlived our usefulness? The desire to serve and to work, and the habit of doing so, has been the pattern of our lives and usually the happy part of our lives. "Where there is no hope there is no duty, no work, nothing to be gained by praying, nothing to be lost by doing only what you like."

Mary Jarrett, in her *Care of the Chronic Sick* (1931), said: "In going from home to home, one gets a decided impression that where there is an attempt to fill profitably the leisure time of the guests, there is less complaining and a more wholesome attitude towards life."

Six homes for the aged in New York City, with the coöperation of the Welfare Council conducted an experiment in 1930–1932 with the object of creating occupation under instruction for old people in homes of the aged, selling the articles produced in the open market, and providing the workers with pin money. It was recognized at the start that this goal was different from occupational therapy, the value of which has been known to so many institutions for the sick and handicapped. This was a distinct attempt to make marketable articles and to avoid the fairs and sympathy sales which have been resorted to by many agencies as the sole means of disposing of their products.

The Committee believed that if competent designers and instructors were provided, old people could make salable articles and could find great interest in so doing. They foresaw variables with regard to the degree of participation of different homes, and of the same home at different times in the year.

Obvious among these variables are the physical conditions in the homes, the ages and physical conditions of the members, their social, intellectual, economic, and work background, and the institutional activities. But primarily, participation depends on the deep and abiding interest, the skill, ingenuity, and salesmanship of those directly in charge.

Institutional activities, the carrying on of the various services of the home, kitchen, laundry, office, etc., have always been considered as legitimate and normal work opportunity for members of homes, at times offering the only kind of work within the interest and capacity of the individual. It is always taken for granted that no work is prescribed or permitted without the approval and supervision of a doctor or his qualified representative.

Some years ago the superintendent of a municipal sanitarium, who believed in work therapy but had no opportunities other than work connected with the daily routines of the institution, plotted out a series of part-time activities that included most of the household and many of the nursing and other medical services. His successor not only carried on, but found he could do the work of the institution at a lower per capita cost. Slowly we began to get stories that even patients with slight temperature were permitted to work, for otherwise the activities of the institution would be neglected and the welfare of many patients endangered. One day the Commissioner of Health, visiting the sanatorium, found one of the patients carrying from the dining room buckets of silver weighing over 30 pounds each. In no uncertain terms he made it known that the sanatorium was run for the benefit of the patients; the latter were not there to aid in the economical operation of the institution.

Work by patients or guests at a home as a normal interest in the place in which one resides and an expression of appreciation, or as therapy with limited money value, is one thing. Activities essential to the conduct of an institution, and ordinarily performed by regular paid employees is something else again. In the first instance it is a form of therapy and the question of compensation need not arise, whereas in the second it is work of a type that is as truly an operative cost as the operation of the heating or lighting of the home.

In connection with the question of compensation as a form of incentive and its relationship to occupational therapy, Dr. S. Wachsman when he was medical director of Montefiore Hospital told the following story. A child was observed to be taking cod-liver oil so cheerfully that a lady asked why he took it with such evident relish while other children generally made faces. The child said, "Yes, but I am getting a nickel every time I take my oil." "I see," said the lady, "And what do you do with all that money?" "Oh," said the child, "When I have saved up enough my mother buys me a new bottle of cod-liver oil."

There probably would be no disagreement that work therapy as well as occupational therapy should be purposeful; that it should have standards of beauty, of workmanship, of utility, and if possible, of all three. Considerable progress has been made since the days when the selection and styling of articles was such that they not only had no sales value, other than sentiment, but must have failed in their primary purpose of giving joy and satisfaction to the people who made them. In the homes as well as in the hospitals we find men and women severely disabled, sometimes compelled to work in prone positions, making articles that are as artistic as they are utilitarian.

In any discussion of compensation as an incentive in work therapy with the aged, we find that most people emotionally are either for or against paying the members of the home, even when we consider only articles that are sold.

Those for compensation urge: If we believe in work therapy, then we want the largest participation possible. Most people need some incentive, and to men and women with little or no income, some compensation is such an incentive. It is better to earn money than to depend on a spending allowance from the institution. Among those who would not participate without compensation are guests who for their own welfare and that of the home need it most. Articles made and sold are priced considerably higher than the cost of material and therefore include labor. While occupational or work therapy necessarily operates at a deficit, clients' work should not be appropriated as an offset to such loss. In some institutions the client pays the cost of material. He keeps the completed article or sells it for whatever price he can get. Others divide the difference between cost of materials and selling price, or that portion which they feel represents labor costs among all clients participating, on the basis of hours worked. Still others believe strongly that compensation should be based on the part played by the individual in creating the value of the finished article, comparable to a piece or production rate.

Those opposed to compensation urge: If the guests can be induced to participate because of a desire to do something for themselves, for the home in which they live, or for others—such participation is at a much higher level than if it is based on compensation, which is an artificial incentive. Without an artificial stimulant, all activity is voluntary and avoids any air of compulsion. Some old people are skillful and retain a fair degree of dexterity, while others are slow and can do simple work only. If low production is due to physical limitation, such handicapped persons deserve more credit, but would get less compensation. These factors would make it difficult to arrive at a satisfactory compensation and would lead to injustice or discrimination. If the actual earnings are too low, the purpose of incentive is defeated, and a sense of inferiority is created. Working without pay gives guests a sense of participating or making a return to the home for care received.

Recently I visited one of the homes in New York where there is no compensation for the guests. In the occupational therapy department some of the guests were preparing bandages for one of the large voluntary hospitals and were told that this work was their contribution. Others were engaged in making a variety of articles that were to be sold. Of the 327 guests, 157 worked in the occupational therapy department and on other activities. Of the 170 remaining, 69 were not able to work because of some disability; 61 percent of the guests physically able to work took part in some activity at the home.

Mrs. Florence W. Switton, at the National Conference of Social Work, Seattle, 1938, said:

> We recognized the value of activity over passive entertainment. Subsequently we came to a realization that our general program could be greatly improved by injecting therein a new motivation.
>
> We found from our actual experience that if the activities of the aged person were not only recreationally enjoyable or culturally stimulating, but were linked to a practical or economic use, the psychological benefit would be enhanced. The essence of the matter is that activity which is economically useful provides a satisfaction and sense of real living—of earning one's keep. In brief, the addition of the economic motif to activity of old age is as valuable psychologically in homes for the aged as it is normally beneficial to life in general. . . .
>
> Again we sound a warning that such activity is intended solely for the benefit of the individual and not for the benefit of the institution. . . .
>
> Members of old age homes were surprised that they were capable of renewing their formerly useful lives. Once realized, the idea brought them renewed zeal for living. . . .
>
> Our experience convinced us that a program based on the foregoing principles is applicable to any home for the aged, provided only that it be sufficiently individualized and adapted to the particular economic outlets available and to the aptitudes of the residents.
>
> Remember, however, we deal with a mentally despondent and physically dilapidated group of weary old people. They must be studied and sympathetically and patiently nursed into such a program. It is a slow and tedious process and is based on maximum effort, understanding, interest, and zeal and an inspirational desire to serve.

Sometime we find a person who does not want occupational therapy. One man I know has his book and pipe and doesn't want to be bothered with anything else. The occupational therapist sometimes does reach the point where he does not know how to get a response. The founder of a model home project once described to me the devices he had to use in order to gain the coöperation of tenants in keeping their homes in good condition. Many of these people did not know how to take care of their quarters and when these became uninhabitable would seek residence elsewhere.

Similarly the occupational therapist must try all sorts of dodges so that persons who do not want occupational therapy may be exposed to projects in which they could become interested.*

In every home there are people who like to stay alone in their own rooms when working on a particular project. There are others who work in solitary fashion practically all the time. Older persons who live by themselves in homes and who are not inclined to mix should be left alone and not forced to join in with the others, providing they are happier by themselves. On the other hand, they may be waiting for someone to draw them out, and be thankful when this happens. The important thing is to find out to what extent the person who works alone likes or dislikes this. A woman that I know in one of the old age homes has a very real reason to prefer solitude, but sometime when she is thrown in with a group she "mixes." When nothing occurs to bring her together with people she remains alone and likes that too.

If a person follows some form of occupational therapy by himself, that will not necessarily make him more isolated. Sometimes a man feels so inferior that he likes to be left alone. If he is allowed to work off tensions in solitude and live out his daydreams that way,

* *Editor's Note:* Edward Hall, director of the Universal School of Handicrafts, when presented with a new student asks the latter to walk around his studio. As he does so, Mr. Hall watches him very closely and notes where the student's eyes seem to linger the longest, especially where he pauses to examine tools and objects. Even though the newcomer feels there is nothing which definitely interests him and even though he is unaware of where he is pausing the longest, each one of us does have unconscious preferences and we give ourselves away to a skillful observer. Mr. Hall often has talked about arranging a desk full of samples in which every possible object in a handicraft studio might be available in miniature form so that the newcomer could try himself out.

There is one additional device which occupational therapists might use with persons unresponsive to their offerings. These are the various "interest schedules" developed by psychologists which quickly reveal the things that people like to do.

he may get himself in hand so that he will be more relaxed and amenable when he mixes later on with people.

A male member of an old age home who kept to himself was asked why he did not talk to others. He answered that he preferred to talk to himself because then he knew he was talking to a gentleman. Such a remark may be indicative of misanthropy, mild eccentricity, or a mental derangement. If we make such a man feel he has worth-while qualities and can contribute something important to the group, he may lose his fear of people and allow himself to be socialized. Occupational therapy can make an antisocial person less so. When such an individual joins a group he is compelled to become more social, at least temporarily.

Since occupational therapy brings people together working in similar groups, it will facilitate social relations between men and women and this in turn may lead to romantic friendships and marriage. The main purpose of occupational therapy is vocational and emotional rehabilitation. But sometimes a device intended for one purpose is used in other ways. So it is here. In old age homes where men and women are allowed to marry and leave the institutions, occupational therapy may be recommended for its marriage-furthering possibilities in addition to all the other values it may have.

The question is often raised as to the use of reading in therapy. In a hospital situation where patients are confined to bed and can engage in little muscular activity, we do not wish to stress reading because they already have all of that which is good for them. Tuberculosis sanitariums, on the other hand, have done much with reading, because the tuberculous cannot have activities calling for exertion. The reading may be of material directed toward a vocational interest.

Dr. Abram Kardiner in his *Psychological Factors in Old Age* sums up the need for occupational and work therapy, when he states that, "For an ideal society we would demand for the aged that their activities should never be abruptly stopped, but changed in accordance with their altered capacities; for as long as the individual is alive, in addition to food and love, he needs the opportunity to be functioning and effective."

TOWARD A SCIENCE OF BIBLIOTHERAPY

By Alice I. Bryan *

THE ASSUMPTION that stimulation received through reading may affect an individual's emotions, attitudes, and subsequent behavior is as old as the art of reading itself. That the effects of reading may be qualitatively good or bad, depending upon the type of material read and the emotional and intellectual maturity of the reader, has likewise been accepted almost as a truism. One of the major techniques of education has been the use of printed materials for purposes of information and instruction. Conversely, the prohibition of certain types of reading materials has been almost as universally practiced as a major form of censorship. Opinions may differ widely and fashions change radically with regard to the specific kinds of material that are judged to be beneficial or deleterious. But the continued practice of these supplementary strategies of prescription and prohibition of reading testifies to an unchanging belief in its power to influence both children and adults.

In attempting, from the standpoint of education, to differentiate between helpful and harmful reading, certain materials will be found to resist this twofold classification. While contributing nothing substantial in the way of useful knowledge, they could hardly be said to exert a pernicious influence. Educators seem agreed that if people find such materials amusing or entertaining, they should not only be permitted but encouraged to read them as a wholesome way of utilizing leisure time. Thus, to the educational function of reading may be added the recreational. Still another function of

* Assistant Professor, School of Library Service, Columbia University, New York. Dr. Bryan's paper originally was presented before the Hospital Libraries Committee, American Library Association, at its annual meeting, June 23, 1939, and was published in the *Library Journal*, October 15, 1939, but its theme is so important to those who deal with the aged, that in abridged form and by special permission, it appears here.

reading may theoretically be differentiated from these. To the extent that the printed word may induce reactions beneficial to the individual's physical or mental health, reading may be said to have therapeutic value. Upon the validity of this assumption rests the possibility of a science of bibliotherapy.

Research is currently being conducted by members of the medical profession who are interested in the interrelationships between emotional states and specific physiological diseases. They are studying various ailments which have not yielded successfully to treatment by mechanical or chemical techniques. Some of these ailments which have a seriously high incidence of mortality and disability have been observed to involve an underlying emotional component. Results of such studies are now appearing in published form in a new scientific journal, sponsored by the National Research Council, *Psychosomatic Medicine.* The principal field of experimentation so far has been in connection with gastrointestinal diseases, cardiovascular diseases, asthma, diabetes, skin diseases, and accidents. It seems probable, however, that many other ailments may upon investigation be found to be related to emotional maladjustments.

That the sick person must be understood and treated as a whole is the thesis of an interesting and important new book by Dr. G. C. Robinson of Johns Hopkins University, entitled *The Patient as a Person,* and published by the Commonwealth Fund. This book describes a series of studies of unselected patients which Dr. Robinson made with the coöperation of the staff of the Johns Hopkins Hospital. He reports in detail the relationships found between the physical ailments of these patients and their social conditions, personal problems, and emotional reactions to factors apparently lying outside the range of physical pathology. Of especial interest are his findings on the significance of poverty, friction in the home, and emotional shock as contributing factors in gastrointestinal disorders and asthma. His case studies also throw light on the social and emotional status of patients with tuberculosis, cardiovascular symptoms, and diabetes. The conclusion drawn by Dr. Robinson as a result of these studies is that sound diagnosis and effective treatment depend upon an understanding of the emotional and social problems of the patient no less than upon the medical history, physical diagnosis, and technical therapeutic procedures.

Let us accept as a working hypothesis the view that physical and mental health are functionally interrelated and that both depend upon the development and maintenance throughout life of a healthy, integrated personality. The field of bibliotherapy might then be defined as the prescription of reading materials which will help to develop emotional maturity and nourish and sustain mental health. This definition broadens the scope of bibliotherapy to include not only the use of reading materials as an alleviative or curative measure for persons already ill, but as a preventive agent to keep people well. This more comprehensive conception is in harmony with the viewpoint of preventive medicine. It is also completely in accord with the objectives of the mental hygiene movement, which stress prevention as a major strategy for decreasing the alarmingly high incidence of mental disorders. Indeed, it would seem that a science of bibliotherapy should be an important instrument for implementing the objectives of a national mental-health program.

In an address in October, 1938, at the twenty-eighth congress of the American College of Surgeons, Dr. Gordon R. Kamman, instructor in neurology and psychiatry at the University of Minnesota, defined bibliotherapy as a form of "psychological dietetics." He amplified this by saying that: "Reading must be prescribed for patients just as their medicines, physiotherapy, occupational therapy, and diet are prescribed."

If we expand his definition to include the prevention as well as the treatment of illness, and add the conception of a scientific approach, we might extend his phrase and define bibliotherapy as "the science of psychological dietetics."

As an example of the type of assumptions which have been offered as guiding principles for applied bibliotherapy, we might examine a few listed by Dr. Eric Kent Clarke, director of the Division of Psychiatry, University of Rochester School of Medicine, in an article on "Books for the Convalescent."

In the early years of his practice Dr. Clarke's method had been to provide sick patients with outstanding books that seemed to him to have real merit and to offer great possibilities for improving the mind. Much to his disgust, however, the books usually remained unread. He describes one such incident: a clergyman who had suffered a fracture entailing a long period in bed was given a rather rare but thoroughly heavy scientific volume which, when well, he had expressed regret that he had been unable to obtain. A few days later the doctor happened in and was chagrined to surprise him in the middle of a Henty book. The clergyman said that the book had been one of his boyhood favorites and that he was rereading it with great enjoyment. He then apologized, in a tone bristling with guilt, because he had not found time to touch the doctor's contribution. As a result of such experiences, Dr. Clarke offers the following rule: "Underestimate rather than overestimate your reader's intelligence in the sick room and your range of selection will meet with better approval." An analogous rule is: "Do not try to use the convalescent period as an opportunity for education, unless the illness is a prolonged one and the reader specifically asks for it."

The two rules quoted above actually tell us nothing of the effects upon convalescents of reading materials designed for intelligent adults. All we know is that his patients rejected the books he selected for them when he attempted to educate them by improving their minds. One patient felt guilty because he had not been inclined to sample the doctor's gift before the latter's next visit. Was this perhaps because the doctor, who by his own admission had secured the book and borne it to the patient with anticipation of gratitude for his trouble, had shown his chagrin at finding the clergyman happily occupied with a book of an entirely different type? We must admit the possibility that the lack of response from his convalescent patients to the doctor's educational efforts might have been due to the ineffectiveness of his pedagogical technique rather than to the inability of the patients to profit from education. A different response might have been obtained if the book selection as well as the method of presentation had been based upon the readers' psychological needs and interests instead of upon the traditional concept of mind training.

Dr. Clarke related the story of a patient on whom he pressed a book of P. G. Wodehouse's which had impressed him greatly as a unique bit of humor. The central situation reminded the patient of the careless motorist who had knocked him down, and he found the book a terrible bore. A few days later the same patient showed a much cheerier response to a gruesome murder mystery by S. S. Van Dine. "As a result," says Dr. Clarke, "humorous volumes must be regarded as unreliable. They are all well worth trying, but don't be disappointed if they fail to score." We might raise the question here as to whether it was the humorous style of the book or merely the unfortunate associations of the plot which irritated the reader. If we are to have a science of bibliotherapy, we must pass beyond the anecdotal stage in formulating principles and proceed to scientific experimentation.

Dr. Kamman, in the speech referred to previously, mentioned the need for close coöperation between the physical and the bibliotherapist. He urged that specially trained hospital librarians be made available for consultation with the hospital staff, and that the surgeon try to use the services of such librarians just as he now uses trained dieticians to plan a patient's treatment. He recognizes that "it requires experience, training, and skill to fit the right book to the right patient."

It seems obvious that a thorough knowledge of human psychological adjustments would be equally valuable, if not indispensable, for the bibliotherapist. He should also have an understanding of the newer concepts of educational philosophy and methods. In the final analysis, the building of any science depends upon the ability and training of the men and women who devote their lives to its development. The question "Can there be a science of bibliotherapy?" may be answered in the affirmative. Whether there will be, within our lifetime, depends upon the answer which these men and women give.

OCCUPATIONAL THERAPY

By Marguerite Emery *

OCCUPATIONAL THERAPY is not a new idea, for in 172 A.D. Galen, the great Greek physician and philosopher wrote "employment is nature's best physician, and is essential to human happiness." Down through the ages wise physicians have always advocated the healing power of work as an aid to convalescence for both young and old. In 1791 the Frenchman Pinel suggested not once but many times in his papers that a combination of work and exercise would be of value in the treatment of the mentally sick.

But although this theory was recognized and used by individual doctors, it was not until the beginning of the nineteenth century (in 1815, in fact) that definite steps were taken in this country to organize a work program. At that time Thomas Eddy, a member of the board of governors of the Society of the New York Hospital wrote a paper which he delivered before that body, urging a carefully worked out program of occupational therapy for the mentally sick. In this he was influenced by the work of Rush, in this country, and the work of Samuel Tuke of the York Retreat in England.

In spite of the vision and intelligence displayed by Tuke and in spite of the fact that this program was put into effect with success, occupational therapy did not gain much headway in this country, except in isolated spots, until the First World War. After our entry into the war, the government, watching the effects of hospitalization upon men in England, Belgium, and France, took the steps already initiated in these countries to offset the harm.

* At present Director, Occupational Therapy Department, Neurological Institute, New York City. The writer presented this paper while Chief Occupational Therapist at Mt. Sinai Hospital. Since the audience for the lectures upon which this book is based consisted of people living in or around New York City, the material of the present discussion was limited to such a group and did not cover the subject as a whole.

This problem of hospitalization was an acute one. Here were men, young men, middle-aged men, men prematurely aged by war, obliged to stay in hospitals for periods varying from a few weeks to months, and even in some cases years. Men with facial disfigurements waited six months between plastic operations. Included in this group were the so-called shell-shocked and men with obstinate wounds which refused to heal. Some of these men were in bed for months at a time, but many were ambulatory, free to wander about the wards and the grounds with nothing definite to do and no responsibilities from morning to night. The problem was not unlike that presented in any home or institution for the old. How could one keep these men in a healthy state of mind, renew their ambition, keep up their morale, release tension and prevent deterioration?

The government recognized this problem, gathered a small group of women trained in crafts and in handling people, and sent them overseas. These women were given the title of "reconstruction aides." Under this title came also the physiotherapists with their exercises and massage. The name "reconstruction aide" covered all occupational therapists, whether or not they were engaged in the educational, recreational, or work aspects. This small and valiant group, which had been sent overseas as an experiment, did so well that General Pershing cabled for two hundred more. As time went on and the activities became better established, workshops were set up in hospitals, some equipped with elaborate tools and machinery and some with not much more than willing hands and a strong desire to be of service. Not content with the shops, the reconstruction aides carried the work to the bedside of the patients. In their enthusiasm they carried it everywhere, and many a man ordered to the prison ward for some misdemeanor was much surprised to find his therapist waiting for him with his work! Besides having crafts at which they could become remarkably proficient, the men were able to carry on their education, or learn to sketch and paint under competent instructors, all of which helped bridge the gap between army and civilian life. In the larger hospitals, where long-time cases were looked after, it became possible for a man to occupy all his waking hours in a program consisting of study, diversion, and work. And to the credit of the average soldier it must be admitted that the great majority took advantage of this opportunity, officers too, from colonels to lieutenants, made use of the chance to occupy their time. And so, when the last step came—discharge from the army—it proved an easy one for the men to accept, since they had already established work and study habits and were ready to meet their responsibilities.

The profession of occupational therapy took a long step forward at the end of the war, as hospitals and sanitariums became increasingly aware of the value of this service. Various specialists began to appear, first in the field of mental diseases and in tuberculosis sanitariums, then in connection with orthopedic and spastic difficulties and in cases of children with cerebral palsy. Schools of occupational therapy were established and high standards set. Anyone who now desires to write O.T.R. (Occupational Therapist, Registered) after her name must be a graduate of one of the five schools recognized by the American Medical Association. The present requirement is three years of intensive work with plenty of fieldwork.

Active occupational therapy departments now exist in such diverse places as mental hospitals, homes for the aged, homes for incurables, hospitals for joint diseases, mental hospitals, tuberculosis sanitariums, state schools, and prisons. In New York City alone there are twelve occupational therapy departments under city management. Flourishing departments exist at Bellevue, King's County, Sea View, Metropolitan, Cancer Institute, Welfare Hospital, City, the Municipal Sanatorium at Otisville, Bellevue Psychiatric, and Riverside, as well as at such homes for the aged and infirm as the City Home on Welfare Island and the Farm Colony on Staten Island.

In the general hospitals scattered throughout the country, the work falls under two heads, the functional and the diversional. In the functional the aim is to restore stiff muscles, aid circulation, and gradually strengthen weakened parts by increasing doses of work, all carried out under a physician's watchful eye. Bellevue Hospital, for instance, has a really excellent department for functional work. Airplane injuries, as well as automobile accidents, fill the modern hospital with fractures and bone injuries. The functional work of the occupational therapist has progressed so rapidly that in certain localities, insurance companies send their disabled workmen to occupational therapy workshops for treatment. A striking example of this procedure is the model Junior League Workshop in Milwaukee, where highly trained therapists work with insurance cases, and with spastic children. The period of disability is shortened, the worker's hope and morale is kept up, and his desire to reënter industry is strengthened through these treatments.

In London, at the present time, occupational therapists are working with children crippled in air raids. "We cannot afford to wait," they say, "we have to start rehabilitating them before it is too late." These therapists work in the shops all day, and drive ambulances when necessary at night.

The diversional or recreational work of the general hospital is very heavy because of the rapid turnover in these hospitals. It is much more important than it seems on the surface. It is surprising to see how quickly patients calm down under the steadying influence of work. "It takes my mind off of things" is the almost universal remark. The middle-aged and the old are quite as insistent upon occupational work as the younger people, and much thought is expended upon projects that they can master easily in a short time, without too much strain.

Anyone who has watched the intense anxiety of patients before operations will realize the value of a work project that keeps patients busily occupied in the hours preceding an operation and puts work in their hands as soon as they are able to sit up. The work must be colorful, gay, and easily accomplished.

In a certain hospital a man was confined to a ward for weeks and finally months. The head nurse came to the therapist and asked that he be given work. His irritability, restlessness, and worrying was interfering with his treatment and, incidentally, it was affecting the other patients. "He drives us all crazy," she said. Under an occupational therapy program suited to him and administered daily, he calmed down, spending as much time as he could in the occupational-therapy workshop. While he chose his own tasks, he was guided tactfully to long-time projects because of his drive to finish short ones quickly. On his bad days he was very apt to destroy the work over which he had labored for a long time, so upon those days he was encouraged to plan patterns for new projects, instead of working on actual material. His age, illness, and decidedly neurotic make-up all had to be taken into consideration in dealing with him.

Still another man, prematurely aged by a frightful experience in Germany where he was beaten up and left for dead by the Storm Troopers, was admitted to the workshop for functional work in an effort to restore some power to his paralyzed arm and hand. Although it did not help the patient in this respect, he enjoyed it so much and was so greatly benefited by it in other ways, that the treatment was prolonged for months. The change twice a week from a lonely room to a congenial atmosphere did much for him, and in spite of his cultural background, he took great pride in the fact that his very considerable disability did not prevent his making useful and attractive trays and baskets.

The convalescent patient also needs work to keep him or her contented during a prolonged hospital stay. And the diabetic patient must have his great energy diverted into healthful channels during a hospital stay.

So strongly entrenched is occupational therapy in mental hospitals that it seems impossible to think of one without it. New York State has many hospitals with large O.T. staffs. Much of the progress of work therapy is due to their vision. Two out-patient psychiatric clinics in this city have occupational therapy departments attached to them; they are Vanderbilt Clinic and Mt. Sinai Hospital. The department of the latter is the pioneer in the field and takes care, during the morning, of psychiatric patients of both sexes and all ages referred from the clinic. These patients choose their own work and by so doing help to work out their own conflicts. Finger painting as therapy and as an aid to treatment is carried on.

Reëstablishing habits of regular attendance and definite work periods and activities helps these people get back into normal life, while the feeling of shelter that the hospital affords is of great benefit during this time. "The aim of the occupational therapist," one psychiatrist states, "is to find some level at which the patient's energies, poorly organized as they sometimes are, can be directed into channels of real activity. By this means dormant interest can be awakened and phantasy replaced by satisfying work and recreation."

A mixed group is of great value, since it stimulates the interest of many to have this chance at normal relationships and paves the way for recreational work. Even when the conduct of some of the patients leaves much to be desired, a mixed group has a distinct advantage over a one-sided one. Dr. C. P. Oberndorf stresses this point in an article entitled "Sublimation in Occupational Therapy": *

> As far as possible there should be no segregation of the sexes in recreation or in work, the object being to offer the members of both sexes opportunity, no matter how tenuous, for mutual direct emotional expression. It is possible, even probable, that certain incidents which may be annoying to the therapist will occur. Still the aim of occupational therapy is to absorb emotional effect in direct or sublimated form and not to frame a peaceful picture of an obedient group in enforced tranquility. The degree to which sublimation can be carried by normal individuals is variable, but in the majority it is distinctly limited, and when sublimation fails one finds either a regression or a perversion, an emotional outburst of an intense nature, a complicated compulsion or a marked anxiety state.

In 1925 the Mt. Sinai Clinic tried the experiment of giving the psychiatric patients a party at a neighboring settlement house. This proved a great success. So important was this get-together to the patients, that two parties a year were held thereafter. At the end of two years, a weekly club was started and this has been in existence ever since. It would take too long to tell how the club broadened to include first the older women, and then all ages. It is an inspiring sight to see these repressed, mentally sick people expand in a congenial atmosphere, each having his own little place in the sun. At these meetings there is no set program, each chooses what he or she prefers to do, whether it be ping-pong, Chinese checkers, cards, bagatelle, etc. Simple refreshments, consisting of icecream, cake,

* *Occupational Therapy and Rehabilitation*, XI (June, 1932) 155–65.

and hot chocolate, are much appreciated and it is astonishing to see how normally the "patients" behave.

Once during every summer a picnic is held to which the patients are taken in busses, seventy-five or eighty strong, in ages ranging from thirteen to seventy years. Special parties are also given at Thanksgiving, Christmas, and in the spring. This program is under the Occupational Therapy Department, since work and pleasure are so closely allied.

"Not to work is to die," says one philosopher, and this seems particularly applicable to the old. Accustomed to active, useful lives, they are miserable and unhappy without work. In farsighted homes and institutions, occupational therapy plays an important part. Here people have plenty of time, all the time there is: time for the men to make stunning toys which take hours of sanding and polishing, painting and assembling. Time for women to weave and do beautiful bargello work, to make bags and chair seats of fine tapestry, to embroider linens and to hook rugs that are worthy of a place in a museum. One home sets aside all weaving activities for blind residents. Intricate carving is often a product of these workrooms, but a wise therapist stresses not so much the excellence of the result, as the fact that all may participate in such a project.

It is always possible to find something for everyone to do, and sometimes it is possible to pay small sums to these people for their work. Constructive activity turns thoughts outward into wholesome channels, therefore workrooms should be cheerful, happy places. One of the most important results is the socializing effect of people's working together.

In what we hope will be the near future, work for the homebound will be just as necessary and as customary as medical and nursing care. Such a program was tried in New York City years ago under an organization called the "Fraternity for Friendly Service." It filled a long-felt want before it was forced by the depression to disorganize.

The crippled or cardiac child, the sufferer from tuberculosis, and all other homebound individuals will have work brought to them as a matter of course, and a really adequate program will be arranged to take care of the elderly man or woman living at home or in lodgings who are well, strong, and anxious to do something that will relieve the monotony of life.

Only recently a young woman telephoned to ask how to get occupational therapy for her invalid mother, a cardiac case suffering from a slight stroke and homebound. The doctor wished the patient to be occupied and the anxious daughter did not know how to provide simple occupation.

The occupational therapist of the future will be able to visit the homebound, and bring them work and new projects at least once a week, for as every trained worker knows, someone must direct and administer this therapy. It is useless to start a project and expect an individual to continue without hope and encouragement. And it is perfectly feasible to have central shops where the articles made by old people can be sold. When this happens it will be occupational therapy's contribution to the problem of growing old.

THE CREATIVE URGE IN OLDER PEOPLE

By Edward T. Hall *

CHARLES DICKENS in *The Tale of Two Cities* uttered a bit of philosophy that might well be used as a text for this article: "You see," said Doctor Manette, "it is very hard to explain, consistently, the innermost workings of this poor man's mind. He once yearned so frightfully for that occupation, and it was so welcome when it came; no doubt it relieved his pain so much, by substituting the perplexity of the fingers for the perplexity of the brain, and by substituting, as he became more practised, the ingenuity of the mental torture; that he has never been able to bear the thought of putting it quite out of his reach."

Man is naturally creative. He finds peace and satisfaction when he expresses this urge by making things with his hands. Unfortunately, our educational system and manner of living in America have not emphasized the vital importance of such expression in a well-ordered life. Back in 1905, when Das Gupta founded a weaving school in the home of the late Rabindranath Tagore in India, Mahatma Gandhi stated that everyone, irrespective of his station in life, should devote at least one hour of every day to doing something creative with his hands.

The urge for individual expression may be submerged or lie dormant during a long life. Apparently, however, this creative spark remains alive and under proper handling may be fanned into a flame. Our studies with thousands of people of all ages suggest that each person has preferences as to mediums of expression.

A man who was well on in years came into the school one evening to look around. He explained he had too much time on his hands, was bored with movies, cards, and life in general. He had been an

* Director and Founder, Universal School of Handicrafts, New York City.

executive and had never used his hands. He didn't know what to do. I told him to wander through the different studios to see what others were doing. As the bee is drawn to the lotus, we found him intently watching a younger executive in the clay room. We brought him a smock so he could play there. As the weeks passed he and his friends were surprised by the high quality of his work, which later we, in fact, put on exhibition.

Another retired business man browsed around the school for an hour or so and then said, "I want to learn how to weave." It was new to him, and he had never realized that it would appeal to him. Today, he is a fine weaver and enjoys the satisfaction of creating for his family and friends fabrics they deeply appreciate.

A seventy-three-year-old lady knew definitely what she wanted to do when she inquired whether there was an age limit for students. Pounding in copper had appealed to her since early married life. Now as a grandmother, she had her first opportunity to follow that urge. She was with us every day for several months, doing excellent work. She is now head of a creative department in a private girls' school. Welcome Lawson was seventy-six and nearly blind when he enrolled to learn how to make copper ash trays to sell to Vassar College students. He had been a lawyer.

Two executives, who will shortly be forced to retire, have mastered weaving of yardage fabrics for suits. Many of my own tweeds were woven by a white-haired old gentleman; part of the yarns were spun and dyed by an eighty-one-year-old lady. This past week an aged man enrolled in bookbinding and asked for special training in gold decorations.

Helping elderly people discover their chosen creative field is very important. In the Universal School it is simplified because so many distinctly different activities are carried on where they may be observed. No one can predict what a visitor will favor.

One grandmother, who is determined never to grow old, worked in both the leather and pewter studios. She now has her own shop in her home, where she is profitably busy making articles on special order only, mostly for gifts. Another woman, in her late sixties, studied jewelry and developed a series of twelve birthday bracelets for graduation presents. Another little widow, who was old in spirit and well on in years came to the school to get her mind off the crushing sadness of losing her only son. Weaving appealed to her and provided the needed occupational therapy. She soon began to sell her work. The transformation surprised everyone. She now looks fifteen years younger.

Adding creative expression to one's daily routine has a deep and far-reaching effect on the individual. The medical profession uses occupational therapy in both mental and general hospitals to give the human mechanism an opportunity to regain health. Preventive therapy is even more effective. It is especially needed with older people who may lack the will to live possessed by those still in harness. As suggested above, the effectiveness of the activity is greatly increased when we discover what the person would love most to do.

Mr. R. W., a man in his late sixties, had suffered a stroke and was forced to give up his congenial business activities. Realizing that he was merely awaiting death, he became extremely neurotic and started drinking heavily. The psychiatrist whom he consulted, instead of sending him to an institution, decided to place a ready warped loom with yarns and shuttles in the living room one night after his patient had retired.

The next day R. W. began to play with his new toy. He stopped drinking and became his fine, normal self. For several months he wove fabrics for various members of the family and steadily improved physically. Contrary to medical predictions, his heart stopped troubling him, and he has now returned to his business.

To R. W.'s life was added what might be called "Vitamin V in human behavior," bringing results that even science is hard put to explain. R. W. discovered his creative self through happy activity that occupied both the mind and the hands. When the results of these satisfying moments evoked praise from others, R. W. received the ego recognition we all crave. It introduced into the day a reason for living and into the anticipated tomorrow the joy which comes from having completed one's daily task.

Another student at the school was ninety when he and his wife enrolled. They lived in New Hampshire and planned to have a gift shop in their home, which later materialized, most of the articles for sale being fashioned by the elderly couple.

The following winter he returned to the school with blueprints of a new home. He wanted to make a miniature model so they could see just how it would look when completed. He was one of the most ambitious students in the school, and just refused to grow old.

Articles fashioned with our hands are our personally created children. In many lives they fill the gap left by actual children or friends who have drifted away or have disappointed one. An elderly person who has lost initiative and broods over imaginary or real wrongs must be given a happy, effective antidote that gets him out of the grooves of his own thinking, pulls him off the shelf, and provides congenial work. The rediscovery of one's creative self does that—Vitamin V in human behavior.

MENTAL DISEASES OF THE AGED

By Samuel W. Hartwell *

Physicians by lengthening the average span of life have given us more old people and, incidentally, have made it more probable that we too will be old some time. Changing situations and customs have for some time been reducing the birth rate; and so, there are fewer young—as compared to old—people in the world to take care of the aged and to think about how best to do so.

Even in considering young people in terms of their mental health or lack of it, it is very hard to say where mental disease begins. In fact, it is impossible to do so in most cases. Much more is it difficult to do so with the aged, in whom there are always changes in the mental functions incident to or parallel with changes in the physical functions.

It happens that one of the physical conditions, high blood pressure, that is to some degree present in most old people and often causes or relates itself to the appearance of mental symptoms, is one of the diseases that medical science has as yet been able to do little about. Circulatory diseases now stand in first place both as the cause of death and as to prevalence among the general population, both young and old. The result of this is that if we were to compare 1,000 old people of today with 100 living fifty years ago, we would find that of diseases incident in the two groups; cancer, tuberculosis, chronic infections, digestive diseases, and many others would show a marked decrease in the fifty-year period. Cardiovascular conditions would not be decreased, however, in fact numerically they would be increased, and comparatively they would be tremendously increased. This is one of the things that makes the problem under discussion particularly important.

* Professor of Psychiatry and Mental Hygiene, School of Medicine, University of Buffalo.

There is another situation that is becoming more significant for social and institutional workers all the time. The science and art of psychiatry and its allied fields have accomplished something, and have promised much more, in the fields of psychotherapy and of mental hygiene. The public has been led to believe that there are things which may be done to prevent, arrest, and even cure many mental diseases. We are justified in this education, and it is best that the public take this hopeful attitude. However, mental hygienists may not have been careful enough to explain that as yet we know but little about preventing or curing the types of mental diseases that most commonly (we may say almost exclusively) affect the aged person. Perhaps also mental hygienists have not been hopeful enough about this possibility themselves and have therefore not accomplished as much as they might have otherwise. But when the senile mental symptoms begin to appear, friends turn to psychiatrists and social workers for help much more than formerly because they have faith in them and pin their hopes on what mental hygienists may be able to do.

The most immediate and dynamic reason that the problem of mental illness of the aged is much in the thoughts of many people is, of course, that because of the great overcrowding of our institutions for the mentally sick, a rather general effort is being made in nearly all of the states to discharge or parole old people to their own or to boarding homes. Senile psychosis is the clinical entity that has been for several years largely responsible for the increased admission rate of our mental institutions. While senile psychotics generally are considered the cases most easily and safely cared for outside of mental institutions, as individuals they are often very difficult to manage or even socially dangerous to have in the home or community in view of present-day facilities and attitudes.

It is of parenthetical interest to observe that while between 18 and 19 percent of all cases committed to mental hospitals in the United States are diagnosed as senile psychotics, only about two thirds of one percent of the space in the ten leading textbooks of psychiatry is devoted to the entire subject of the cause, pathology, and treatment of all types of senile mental disease. Twelve pages is the longest section devoted to the subject and that is in a 1,300-page book. The average length of discussion is four pages and that discussion is largely in terms of brain structure. No space at all is devoted to the prevention of mental disease in the aged.

One may say that there are three general groups of old people who are psychotic. First, of course, there are in any mental institution a rather large number of old people who have grown old there. That is, they have in young or middle life developed a psychosis and are now old and still are suffering from the same psychosis. These mostly fall in the schizophrenic and organic groups. In some cases old age seems to be in a way a cure of psychotic manifestations. Usually these are people who have had recurrent manic depressive attacks that have never been of great length, and after the age of fifty or thereabouts the episodes cease entirely. Incidentally, one should mention the fact that in most cases of neurosis of long standing the symptoms seem to disappear partially or completely at least to become much less bothersome to the patient when old age arrives.

The second group of the elderly psychotics are those who have had a poorly organized personality, or a mild psychosis, if one wishes to use that expression, for many years and who now break down completely, possibly because of the slight organic changes that occur in the brain of everyone who reaches a physiological old age. This is the group that modern psychiatry now recognizes as much larger and more important than was formerly thought.

The third group is made up of the true senile psychotics: those who, in spite of a previously mentally healthy and well integrated personality, develop a mental disease when the physiological changes in the brain and body occur. An interesting fact to recall during this discussion is that while some anatomical changes occur in the brain of all people who reach physiological old age, there is great variation in the amount of change present in different individuals, and, as near as we can tell, changes in the brain vary in the same individual from other body changes. Still more important to remember is the fact there is no close correlation between the amount of organic change, either circulatory or degenerative, present in the brain as reported by the pathologist after autopsy and the degree of intellectual deterioration or personality disintegration present before death. There is of course a rough correlation.

My opinion is that the psychiatrist who has known the senile in life and observed many symptoms is more often surprised to find the pathologist reporting little change than he is surprised to find much pathology with few symptoms. If this is true, it means that our second group, comprising those who have been carrying considerable unnoticed mental pathology during their active period of life and then develop mental disease in later life, is larger than is usually considered.

In general it may be said that most of the psychoses developing in the fifth decade or thereafter have an organic basis or at least an important organic factor. These are mostly, in the present state of our knowledge, believed to be in the brain. The changes in metabolic and endocrine functions and probably in other bodily functions are often if not always factors.

It is true that everybody faces the great probability of experiencing some changes in his mental life with advancing age. These almost universal changes occur much more in the intellectual processes than they do in the field of deep personality integration. Why some old people undergo certain mental changes and remain themselves for the rest of their lives while others progress until the personality itself is completely lost is something we do not know. Until such time as we learn otherwise, it seems reasonable to think that a mind healthy in the broadest sense, functioning through the active part of life, may be some protection against complete mental disintegration in old age.

The general features of a senile psychosis are only a magnification of the ordinary changes that occur to some degree at least in every person physically old. All of the reasons why some people grow physically old at fifty-five and others at ninety, or why these magnifications are so much greater in one person than in another, we do not know. But there are many theories: physical, dietetic, endocrine, and physiological.

The one factor we are certain is important in many cases is the factor of inheritance. There is in every individual an inherited tendency for or against the early development of the senile arteriosclerotic changes in the brain. In the present state of our knowledge we cannot directly change these inherited tendencies. Some mental hygienists believe that we can perhaps defend ourselves and help others defend themselves against these manifestations by the manipulation of other social, mental, and environmental factors that add strain and stress to the living of one who has a tendency to an early senility. The well-adjusted aging person is often able to plan for the approach of senility, and to help our aging people do this is one of the great tasks of the social worker and the mental hygienists.

It is true that brothers and sisters very frequently show a great similarity in the age at which they show senile changes. This is true both of families showing very late as well as those showing very early changes. But like many other dominant physical traits, it is not the constant rule.

The general symptoms of mental old age are a progressive impoverishment of mental resources (memory being most and usually first affected) and the gradual weakening and "flattening out" of the personality as it is manifest by its reactions to and in the environment.

To describe this in terms of behavior one can say there is a lessening of activity, especially planned activity; a lack of acceptance of new ideas; and a feeling of being left out, which of course is always based in some measure on reality. Memory is poor; one of the first signs of a breakdown of personality is the loss of a realization that memory is failing. Memory for recent events is lost first; the patient is more unable to handle abstract ideas than concrete situations. In a great majority of senile psychotics the personality deterioration is not so marked or its progress as continuous as is the disintegration of the more strictly thought or intellectual functions.

The patient resents any interference, particularly by younger people, and sees no reason why he should not dictate, especially to the younger members of the family. Affections turn to suspicion and even hatred. The patient does not wish to remain with those he suspects or hates. Altruistic and benevolent interests are apt to be lost or blurred. Childish behavior appears, and often the weaknesses of childhood that have been controlled through active life, either through unconscious repression or conscious restraint, will appear openly in the manifest personality of the aged person. Irritable response and defense reactions are common. Inhibitions are lost and the restraints that civilization has imposed no longer operate.

In mental hospitals the senile psychotics are divided into several groups. Those placed in other groups than the simply senile are really those whose personality is more broken. And there is a rather close correlation between the prepsychotic personality type or tendency and the type of the senile psychosis. Those classified as paranoid senile are usually of a suspicious, envious, unforgiving temperament. Those regarded as confused seniles are often people who have had many mental conflicts and who have never had a philosophy of life that worked satisfactorily in helping them find a good way of life. The depressed, agitated group are often those who have had a lifelong tendency to swings of mood. And the presbyophrenic or very happy euphoric seniles are nearly always those who have had formerly a perhaps too happy, vivacious, adjustable personality and who were not exacting enough of themselves or others. These, as one can see, would be likely to make up pleasant stories about themselves. This tendency, called confabulation, is the chief characteristic symptom of this group.

Unfortunately, the psychiatrist knows but little of the factors that result in a senile psychosis. He knows nothing that will check or cure the disease in its progress. His function then is to advise and help the relatives of these unfortunate old people and to advise social workers and others who plan and care for them by evaluating each case as an individual who may be or may not be best cared for in this or that way. And finally the psychiatrist may sometimes be of service in helping relatives and society in general understand and face the reality of their problems.

The question is often asked as to whether or not old people are well cared for in mental hospitals. People visiting their aged friends sometimes feel that they are neglected or that they are placed with other patients who make it unpleasant for them. Social workers, aware of the difficulties under which overcrowded hospitals labor, should try to explain this to relatives and friends of the aged patients. Almost all state hospitals are understaffed and since none of the known methods of treatment used for mental cases accomplishes anything for the senile psychotic, it is logical and surely best that the time of the medical staff should be largely occupied with the more hopeful patients.

Relatives when visiting elderly patients in mental hospitals should know this and not expect the physicians to become as quickly and thoroughly acquainted with the patient's condition and circumstances as they would in the case of patients who might be expected to improve. They should understand also that it often happens that quiet seniles are more appropriately placed in wards with deteriorated schizophrenics than they would be with other old people who perhaps are more disturbed than they or who, because they are talkative, tend to disturb one another.

Relatives should remember that seniles almost always are suspicious and that they often report things they believe to be true that are either a product of their disturbed thought or gross exaggerations. They ought to know that old people should have a simple diet and if they are not fed delicacies it does not mean they have been fed inadequately. And they should realize that any particular patient, including their loved one, is likely to disturb others as much as he is disturbed by others.

The great task of social workers and others interested in the care of the aged is to act as the liaison agent between the relatives and the hospital staff. In these days when the subject of home care of the senile is being discussed and advocated, the social worker can help by remaining objective and by always remembering that each case should be decided on its individual merits. When given the opportunity to be heard by the hospital staff, the worker should be able to show that he has made a thorough investigation of the home situation and of the personality and reactions of those on whose shoulders will fall the burden of care of the senile if he is to be kept in or returned to his home. The worker should be careful at the beginning of the development of the disease or at any other time not to overchallenge relatives as to their duty or ability to handle cases at home. Neither should the worker overemphasize the unpleasant parts of hospital treatment to persuade the family that home treatment is best.

On the other hand, the social worker must plan to be the advocate of the old person and remember that old people are often in the way and that more often than any other group in the state hospital they are "railroaded" into institutions, when they are not really mentally sick enough to warrant it. One of the most important and satisfying experiences a worker can have is to take an old person whose mind no longer serves him well and who is not welcome in the place where he is and help him find a home where he will be as contented as possible, whether it be an old age home or something else.

We are greatly in need of institutions where aged people who are mentally deteriorating can be cared for as a segregated group. Private homes, as good places for children and young people to live and develop in, are often made less helpful or even harmful by the presence of old people whether or not their minds are failing them. When this inadequacy reaches a certain point, older people, even if placed in old age homes, create problems that interfere with other residents. I believe it would be a good thing if most of the old age homes had staffs who accepted the fact that mental deterioration is an inescapable part of growing old.

Public institutions have in the past developed after private ones have paved the way by proving their usefulness. I wish we had more private small homes for the non-disturbed senile psychotics. Then I wish we had more private mental hospitals especially for the aged. A few of these, well staffed and well located as to population, would in my opinion soon create a demand and prove their usefulness so well that it would not be many years until the various states would be providing such homes and hospitals for all old people who needed them.

Other contributors to this volume have discussed the advantages to an individual old person as well to his family of residence in an old age home. Therefore, I do not wish to belabor the point.

We must not forget that while we do not have any proof that mental stress *causes* senile psychosis, we can be sure it makes the symptoms worse. For example, an aging grandfather who has $500 of his own money in the bank, is living in the home of his son. If the old gentleman is feeling out of touch with others in the family and commences to think that his son wants the money, and if his son and the others in the family either do wish they could have it to use or, not needing it, scold or laugh at the grandfather for his suspicions, then this old man, is, in my opinion, much more likely to develop into a difficult paranoid senile than he would were he living with people who understand and overlook his suspicions.

I believe that many individuals who are now unsuitable for care in old age homes because of their mental symptoms would have been satisfactory members of these same homes could they have been placed there earlier.

Unfortunately, we do not have as yet definite early criteria of which persons could or could not adjust. However, the one thing that in my opinion gives us some insight into this most useful evaluation is the study of the longitudinal life adjustment of the patient. It is important to know about the individual's integration in active life. If the adjustment and mental health have been good there is a greater probability that the old person will have a quiet senility. Old age is often blamed for things that are due to lifetime personality factors.

To the extent that this is true, it follows that the practice of the principles of mental hygiene would tend to ameliorate if not to prevent senile psychosis. It is also true that the habit of facing reality is a good one which we should all practice and if possible help old persons in our care to practice. It seems to me that old people who have had a hard life keep their mental faculties much better than those who have had an easy one. These people have solved their own problems and have not run away from life—they are better adjusted. In my experience, the person suffers more who has "kidded" himself into thinking he has made a success and has not. The woman who has played bridge all her life and feels that playing bridge is a measure of success breaks down quicker. Many men and women in old age are often forced to work out these problems from which they have been fleeing all their lives. It is much more important to know the critical experiences of an individual in his lifetime, various delinquent incidents, emotional mishaps, evasive mental stunts, for instance, than to get a history of dates, places, etc. How the individual handled life in the past is the best clue to whether he is equipped to face the problems of advancing age. All of us should try to plan our lives so that we are prepared if it is our fate later to become senile to a pathological degree or to have our parents or other elderly relatives become mentally sick in their old age. This is hard to do and not too often done.

I knew a man who had a family of three children and a faithful wife. He had heard that his grandfather had reached a very early senility and had wasted a large fortune. He had direct knowledge of his father, who in late life became senile, divorced his wife, and married another woman—a marriage that turned out to be very foolish and unhappy. This man said to me when he reached sixty-five, "Do you think that might happen to me? Am I likely to go into a dotage when I get old?" I answered that it might happen. Whereupon the man made his will, leaving his property to his wife and children, and then voluntarily had himself declared in need of a guardian. And it was well he did. For a few years later, he made another will leaving his money and property to designing strangers. By that time, however, he had deteriorated enough so that he had forgotten the legal will, and his wife and children, who had through his life been kind and helpful to him, inherited his considerable fortune. This they would have lost if the wise man had not been gifted with foresight.

In dealing with younger people, the more active kind of therapy is to give the persons a feeling of belonging, a feeling that they are loved. This is something that lends meaning to life. We do this for children by associating with them, by identifying them with us. We all need to experience a certain amount of social response to life. We get that through people who do things for us and who love us. Old people, however, feel left out. The idea of psychotherapy in clinics for out-patient care is a very fine thing. To carry it further by teaching people the need of giving understanding and loving care to old people is the finest thing we can do. Dr. Martin in her Old Age Counselling Center helped old people establish faith in themselves. Many people came to her and when they talked with her, Dr. Martin gave them the moods that they needed.*

In order to bring this understanding to older people we must remember our experiences as a child and profit by them. Those rare people who have such a capacity should be set aside for work in such out-patient clinics, and whenever schools of social service establish courses in work with old people, these qualifications for workers should be stressed. Incidentally, so far as I know there is no course offered in any school that deals with the psychological care of the aged. An evening course was offered at Fordham under the title of "The Needs of Older People" in 1940, but because of insufficient registration it was dropped.

Those who are interested in the care and treatment of old people have all made mistakes. We need each other's help to rectify these and to keep us from making more.

Politicians need psychiatrists and social workers to help them avoid the error of trying to solve the taxpayers' problem by urging too strongly that the problem of state hospital overcrowding be solved by overdoing the sometimes very useful plan of returning senile psychotics to their homes or community.

Relatives badly need the aid of psychiatrists and social workers to help achieve an objective attitude when faced with the social and mental conflicts that occur when some aged member of their family becomes mentally ill.

Psychiatrists need social workers if they are to avoid pessimism as to ever being able to do much about this constantly increasing problem. And psychiatrists need social workers and others who care for the aged to constantly point out the reality of the total situation when we are giving advice to relatives about the best

* Since Dr. Martin's death, the Old Age Counselling Center has continued under the guidance of her long-time professional associate Clare de Gruchy. An affiliated center will be opened in New York City in September, 1943.

solution of the problems presented by the individual case. The most skilled psychiatrist can do no more to help the older person acquire understanding and happiness than can a sympathetic social worker or institution staff member acquainted with the inner world of old age.

And staffs of institutions, social workers, and others need psychiatrists to help plan social care, to give what actual treatment might help, and to teach what little they may know and may later learn about the prevention or postponement of senile mental disease.

And the old people need them all: psychiatrists, psychologists, social workers, enlightened staffs of old age homes! It may not be as thrilling a job to be an advocate of an old person as it is to speak for children, but it is certainly more humane and more necessary.

OLD AGE AT THE CROSSROADS

Patterns of Living: In an Institution *

By Mrs. Helen Hardy Brunot †

Webster defines "crossroad" as a road that runs between roads, or as an intersection of two or more roads. "Crossroads" as used here refers to the point (or points) in life when the older person must chart a new course for himself. It includes also the process of weighing out the different choices available to him and listing the positive and negative values in each.

What kinds of problems do old people face when they find themselves at the crossroads of a decision as to their plans for old age? What "patterns of living" are available to the older person? From which of the following schemes of living may he find one which will meet partly or entirely his personal requirements and preferences: living alone in a room or apartment; sharing an apartment with relatives or friends; boarding with a private family; living in a coöperative apartment house; entering a home for the aged, a nursing home, or a home or hospital for the chronically ill? Is it the type of living arrangement itself, or is it the op-

* In its original form this chapter was a panel discussion, and the attempt has been made to retain here the informal or conversational character of the original meeting. Mrs. Brunot as discussion leader presented the main issue and then introduced the following participants: Ollie Randall, director, Special Services Division, Community Service Society, executive secretary, Ward Manor; Maxwell Lewis, superintendent, New York City Home for Dependents, Welfare Island; Marian McBee, New York City Committee on Mental Hygiene, State Charities Association; Mrs. Lois T. Schneider, Federation of Protestant Welfare Agencies; Sheppard Siegal, M.D., Housekeeping Service for Chronic Patients, Works Progress Administration; Mrs. Frederick Donaldson, Presbyterian Home for Aged Women. The Editor, as discussion leader, took part in the concluding discussion.

The Editor is solely responsible for obliterating the individual contributions and recasting the material in its present form, though the resultant transformation has had the aid, coöperation, and approval of Mrs. Brunot.

† Director, Bureau for the Aged, Welfare Council of New York City, during the period of demonstration, 1939–42.

portunities and services which can be had in conjunction with it that is of significance to the old person at the crossroads of such a decision?

Before we can weigh these questions, we must consider the sort of thing that is likely to bring an old person to the necessity of a decision and the kind of thinking that has made him decide to alter his pattern of living. Prominent among these is the fact that many old people find it impossible financially to continue the arrangement in which they have been living. For them, a suitable place to live within their means is basic to any other aspect of a future plan. In the experience of operating agencies, what are predominant reasons that cause older people to seek special and protected ways of living?

From the viewpoint of the public institution financial need must be present, otherwise the person would not be considered eligible for public care. In a survey of admissions during the period January 1 to February 28, 1940, the New York Home for Dependents found that of the 167 cases admitted, 74 were in need of institutional care because they were physically disabled; they came from hospitals and had no place to go during convalescence. Another 46 came because they were destitute and had no home to go to; 16 had been on relief and came to City Home because they couldn't manage on the relief allowances; in 14 cases their families were unable to take care of them financially; there were 8 whose families refused to take care of them because of desertion or alcoholism; 7 came because they were homeless and needed immediate shelter; 2 needed hospital care. Of these 167 cases, 108 claimed they had relatives, 34 had friends: 25 had neither friends nor relatives.

The Housekeeping Service * also deals with cases where the financial problem is present as a condition of eligibility. In connection with the matter of living arrangement, the Housekeeping Service frequently afforded the chronically disabled old person the choice of institutional or home care. It was found that the poorer the accommodations for care afforded in the patient's own

* Housekeeping Service for Chronic Patients, Works Progress Administration project.

home, the more likely was it that institutional care would be preferable.

Some old people cannot go on paying rent in an apartment or room and by entering a congregate home which operates on a minimum monthly boarding plan they lessen their expenses and still retain a sense of being financially independent. Most old people greatly value this feeling of being on their own and not of being a burden on anyone. Many older people will say, "I want to be independent, I don't want to be dependent on my friends, family, church, etc."

The next group of those at the crossroads are the ones who are no longer able to be as active as formerly, who require regular medical or nursing attention or who like to feel it is there when needed.

However, the question of health care enters into the consideration of future living arrangements even for those who are currently well and healthy. Often the person may be relatively young (in the early sixties) but the thing that seems to be pressing him most and the thing that is the greatest threat is the disability he feels may come in a few years. Most people, young and old, think of old age as a period of infirmity. Many old people are searching for a plan that will afford a safeguard against such possible disabilities. They suffer from the nagging fear of becoming ill in the night, or falling, with no one to look after them. They say "I can get along well enough now but suppose I became ill." There also are a few old people who are just tired and want to find some place where the efforts of daily living will involve as little physical exertion as possible.

Probably the next largest group are those who feel a need for some kind of protection; a way of living which would assure them of psychological security. This desire might arise from a family situation in which they are not particularly happy. Some of these threats and uncertainties occur entirely apart from financial difficulties. The Bureau for the Aged often interviewed persons who were just beginning to explore some future plan for themselves. Among these were persons with assured incomes as high as $100 or

$200 a month who nevertheless suffered from considerable anxiety over future plans.

The New York City Committee on Mental Hygiene most often sees old persons whose need for help arises from behavior problems and from the attitudes of families. There is, for instance, the married daughter who has her mother living with her. She says she can manage this comfortably but her husband will not allow her mother to be in the home. Here the problem is not financial but is rather a matter of family relationships. However, strained family associations become more tense as the financial problem increases in severity.

Loneliness and isolation may be the cause for the old person's need to change his way of living. For instance, one home recently accepted a woman of eighty-two who felt she needed to live in an institution where she would have the companionship of others rather than to continue living alone. Old age assistance recipients sometimes apply for residence in congregate homes for the aged, emphasizing their need for protection or group care, rather than financial need alone.

Here is an interesting question in connection with the matter of what old people seek in the way of living arrangements: do they ask for the thing they really want, or do they ask for what they think they should want?

The experience of the City Home is that old people are often reticent in asking for what they want. For example, the City Home established a vocational placement unit in the Social Service Department. It was thought that by questioning the old people directly the Home might find out what they wanted in the way of recreation and other group activities, and then the Home could plan a program geared to the preferences of the residents. It did not work out that way, and the Home finally arranged a scheme whereby it had two delegates from each ward meet once a month, and through these delegates it was finally possible to discover what the residents of each ward wanted.

A great many persons apply to an institution because they do not know what other living situations are available. Sometimes they want to make a change and someone suggests a congregate home. They apply with little thought as to the change they are undertaking. The adjustment involved in changing from living alone or in a small family to a large congregate group such as that of the institution is considerable. When the applicant is asked why he is thinking of this particular arrangement, it is often found that a congregate home is neither what he wants nor what he is likely to adjust to.

The Bureau for the Aged found that older people as well as their families are greatly misinformed about social agency programs —both institutional and public relief. They misconceive what a home can do for them and also misconceive how old age assistance works with reference to living arrangements and supplementary services. Sometimes even those already receiving old age assistance do not know that they may have a doctor visit them regularly as part of their home care or that housekeeping services can be made available to them also. These facilities are very real to the aged. The knowledge that they are available can serve to relieve many old people of the fear of not being able to manage alone in times of difficulty.

The question often arises as to the types of ailments which can be handled effectively in homes for the aged. Many persons, turned down by one home because of physical ailments, apply to others in the hope that somewhere or other they will pass muster and be accepted. Illness can be taken too readily as a means of rejecting applicants for admission to homes for the aged, a situation probably well known to those acquainted with the thinking behind admission policies.

Many illnesses do not necessarily disable the individual to the point where he is no longer ambulatory. For example, some homes now rule that diabetes and pernicious anemia do not warrant rejection. Instead of requiring special foods, the diabetic, regardless of how severe his illness, needs normal food and himself can learn which of the foods on an ordinary tray he may select. As for insulin, that the patient can usually take himself. A pernicious anemia patient also needs no extensive special care and can get along with one treatment a month.

Of course, we all know there has been a change in the attitude of many of the private homes for the aged and that they are eager to install medical programs but are hampered a great deal by lack of finances. Some even have difficulty in providing limited diet kitchens.

Another question in connection with illness that frequently comes up is what happens to a person on old age assistance who is in a private home for the aged when he is taken ill. The home does not receive additional money from the Division of Old Age Assistance to provide this care. Can it give hospital care if it is willing to do so? The answer is that if the home wants to continue keeping the recipient free of charge, there is no objection to that, but if it does not want to do so, the recipient is transferred to the auspices of the Department of Hospitals which pays the money to the home if it meets the requirements of the Hospital Department. For the first three months, the Division of Old Age Assistance will pay the grants, but if the person continues to require institutional care after that period, it would have to discontinue payments. The money then would have to come from the Department of Hospitals or the home.

The problem of providing for the old person living in a rooming house or completely alone or the problem of an old person who needs medical attention when there is no one around is accentuated in the highly urban community, as it is also in a highly rural section. In both cases, the problem is that of isolation.

Are old people living in rural areas less or more happy than those living in the city? It has been said that older people can keep busier doing nothing in the country than they can in the city. Older people who are restricted in their movements frequently find it very pleasant to watch life pass by in front of them without the necessity of their participating in it. In planning housing for the aged in England it was found that older people did not want to live in the secluded courts which were thought especially desirable for them. Instead, they wanted quarters on a street where they could see things happening.

However, the question is not whether old people in general are happier living in this or that environment, but rather which environment provides fewer problems for the particular individual. It is the personal element that matters, the old man or woman's accustomed background, his capacity to be active, physically and mentally, his previous vocational and avocational interests, etc.

Relatives often come to an old age home complaining about a cantankerous, overbearing old man or woman that they would like to see admitted. They expect the institution to remake the overcritical, self-centered, and domineering individual, and look to the home to succeed where relatives have failed.

It is true that sometimes the person who is peculiar in one setting may prove satisfactory in another. A woman came to Home B after having been rejected by Home A. Home B accepted the applicant and found her to make an excellent member. Now Home B in earlier years would not have taken her, for, while not ill enough for commitment to the state hospital, the woman did seem in some ways unsuitable for normal congregate life. However, the home had learned from experience that it might be able to handle the type of personality possessed by this applicant. The home was willing to take the chance and the plan proved successful.

Old age institutions might take such persons on trial. It is true that the private homes relate their physical aspects to a person's background. They try to make their institutions into real homes and they have to be careful in choosing their guests in order to make sure that those selected will form a fairly congenial group.

Old people, like children, often get along with strangers when they cannot do so with their own families. This superior adjustment with strangers may indicate that they are more anxious to make a good impression on their fellow members than on relatives. Perhaps, too, they feel that since they will have to spend the rest of their lives in the home, a place that means safety and care, they must force themselves to be friendly and coöperative. It sometimes happens that a cantankerous individual will seem less so when he lives among people who like him and allow him to talk and to have some influence among them. Some individuals are eager to work with others. Others are unwilling or unable to be coöperative. Certainly where there is no desire to coöperate little can be done.

We should see all sides of a person or situation and never depend entirely on the picture presented by the person who is attempting to make the placement or is seeking information as to the best move to make. Complaining relatives, however, are sometimes useful, for they can reveal much of the old person's attitude toward the family. They also reveal their attitude toward the old person and why he is reacting the way he does. There are many other ways by which we gain some insight into the individual, his personality and his ability to adapt himself to new situations. Principally there is the applicant himself. From a good social history of a person it is usually possible to determine what pattern of living among the ones available is best suited to him.

It comes down to this: when an individual is mentally able to participate in the decision, "the best plan for an old person is his own plan."

OLD AGE AT THE CROSSROADS

Patterns of Living: In the Community

By Ruth Hill *

At the crossroads one finds signs telling travelers that the road ahead may be under construction and that one travels at his own risk, or that there is a through highway leading to a definite destination. In either case, one comes to a full stop and looks right and left at the crossroads and makes a decision about further travel.

These considerations apply as one thinks about the hazards of life itself, as well as to physical journeying. In an old-model car a motorist considers whether it is wise to venture out upon a main highway in the rush period. For safety's sake, as well as for enjoyment of the countryside, he may prefer a less frequented thoroughfare. Here the pace is slower, the going a little rougher on the surface perhaps. But the surroundings may be very natural and enjoyable to one who is geared to the simpler pleasures instead of being bent on a mileage record.

One of the first big adjustments an older person must face is that of loss of work. We see many evidences today of the community's preference for younger people in the labor market. The middle-aged unemployed have a difficult time finding work, and the person past middle age in the sixty-five and older age group has a well-nigh impossible task finding reëmployment or staving off retirement. In the OAA Division, it is the common experience to find applicants who have been out of work for years and who have accepted the community's attitude that they are unemployable because of age alone. Yet an independent man of eighty-one who,

* Associate Director of Public Assistance, in charge of Old Age Assistance, New York City Department of Welfare.

with his wife, has lived upon OAA grants for several years recently told me in glowing terms about the ideas he has for selling articles he proposes writing, thus enabling the city to "take us off your hands" and repay all debts.

This attitude, however commendable, is rare and is unrealistic. Most old people living on relief have adjusted to the inevitability of their not being able to earn again. I presume this is less true of the rural than of the city areas in our country. The first crossroad they have met is likely to be one marked "no more pay checks from this point on." The jolt with which one leaves the smooth pavement of a salary status comes to some with a suddenness that is alarming and should not happen if employers had all the facts in mind. Warnings might be given in the way of easing up an assignment gradually and in the development of certain tasks that older people of good experience could fill. Possibly during the next few years with the draining off of many younger people into the services and into defense positions, this will be a community program possibility.

Decreases in income and adjustments in living arrangement are the commonest of crossroads. These will come from sheer financial necessity, and with each move into cheaper quarters a new adjustment in personal contacts will follow. The "familiar" in a setting becomes clothed with fresh significance and the wrench is a painful move each time because of a sense of bereftness the person has to endure. One finds old people who have clung to old neighborhoods from which all former associates have departed and who are themselves unable to articulate their reasons for remaining. They remind one of the barnacles left above the tide line, slowly drying up but sealing themselves ever tighter to the old habitat.

What social workers in the Department of Old Age Assistance try to effect is an improvement in the avenues of living for the older man or woman, so that the setting may continue to be appropriate to their failing activity. It means great patience and constant sensibility to the practical needs often unrealized by the person concerned.

The decline to a lower standard of living necessitated by accepting public-relief status imposes heavy challenges upon the spirit. I think of a couple accustomed in their palmy days to restaurant eating and to life abroad and in various cities of this country following the man's exciting newspaper assignments. They now occupy a first-floor furnished apartment, eat one meal a day out, and struggle at the ages of seventy-seven and eighty-one with the simple tasks of housekeeping entailed in washing their personal clothing and preparing the two meals a day. Even boarding seems too large a relinquishment of privacy, and the sheltered living in an institution does not attract them. Others, however, used to plain living, are secure in the reliable income from the Division. Some old people who have not previously had security show decided improvement in personality tensions after receiving their grants of OAA. One old woman was very peculiar as long as she continued to earn her living in a precarious way. Once she began receiving a regular income from OAA, she changed and became more normal.

We see many old people who ought to live in a congregate way, where the daily tasks of housekeeping would be slight so far as their own share of responsibility is concerned. This change is hardest to effect in old women who have been housekeepers for a long time and have lived alone the past decade or so. The best help toward such a change is a visit to a proposed home for the aged, or a visit from the intake worker of that home so as to have questions answered. If our homes for the aged had no waiting lists, or if there were a much larger number of homes for older people, especially those wanting a place to live as boarding guests with considerable freedom and privacy, our struggle would not be so difficult or so often futile.

One old lady, a Mrs. Black, has lived alone in a shabby, dark, old tenement for seven years and in the neighborhood for forty years. She is seriously handicapped by high blood pressure, heart trouble, and varicose veins. She cannot stand long. She struggles with a kerosene stove and cannot take the chill from her dark rooms in wintry days. Her health has not permitted her to leave the flat in three years. Mrs. Black epitomizes what the psalmist meant when he spoke of "such as sit in darkness and in the shadow of death, being bound in affliction." The Old Age Assistance doctor calls regularly. A visiting nurse dresses and binds her legs, a housekeeper gives her her services three times a week. One friend and the parish priest are regular callers. She loves her church. The absorbing domestic interest is her old cat. If one suggests a Catholic Home, she retorts, "My next move will be to Brooklyn" and with a twinkle, she adds, "to the cemetery."

Mrs. Black had a nasty fall this winter while at the sink and could hardly get back into bed. Meanwhile, she is a real danger to herself and a fire hazard to the other tenants in the building. It will require concentrated action by all the agencies, the physician, the church, the housekeeping project, the nursing service, OAA, and Catholic Charities to effect her transfer to a private home for the aged. These recipients in private homes for the aged continue to receive our financial assistance until they become helpless and in need of continued attendant and medical care, when they are either transferred to the Department of Hospitals or are kept in the home at the expense of the home.

So-called well recipients often have permanent handicaps like progressive limitation of eyesight or hearing even though they are using glasses or hearing aids which the OAA can supply. They become particularly restricted in their activities and they need assistance in keeping a minimum of social contacts to keep life related to the world we live in.

Sometimes a couple presents just as serious a problem of need for further adjustment in living provisions because neither the husband nor the wife is physically able to carry the responsibility of home making. Take Mr. and Mrs. Lossman, living in a very comfortable sunny four-room apartment on the lower East side, their familiar habitat during their adult lifetime. Their vicissitudes have been the result of ill health, and serious they would be even if the couple were independent financially. Mrs. Lossman has paralysis agitans and for the past month has been bedridden and very demanding in her requests for service. They are devoted to each other. Mr. Lossman is suffering from general arteriosclerosis, malnourishment, and cataracts for which he recently underwent an operation. Two of their children are particularly attentive but have families of young children and have experienced much ill health themselves, so that while they visit regularly, they cannot manage to take both old people into their respective homes. Institutional care for Mrs. Lossman is indicated, but neither old person will consent to a separation. They get along with regular visits from the department physician to Mrs. Lossman and clinic visits and a special diet for Mr. Lossman.

They are now favorably considering entering a home together if they pass the home's investigation and are admitted: one to the infirmary ward, the other to the men's ward. This is a serious adjustment, and the children defer to the parents in the decision, which seems likely to go through if the waiting-list problem can be encompassed. The home has been understanding of the reasons for urgency in regard to acceptance. It is a puzzle indeed to know what solution to suggest except this, when a devoted orthodox Jewish couple is involved, needing hospital care as well as care for an ambulatory person, since the municipal hospitals and city custodial institutions do not observe the dietary laws.

So many of our frail elderly people on old age assistance should have boarding-home care rather than be allowed to struggle along alone. We have no list of boarding homes that are found to be satisfactory and are supervised. The OAA staff has not the time to inspect and continue to supervise such homes, nor do we feel we can safely recommend boarding homes just because we know that one other old person lives there. So we resort to hotels of the cheaper kind, or when fortunate find a vacancy in a congregate home like Tompkins Square House or Guest House, and sometimes refer to nursing homes if nursing care is necessary. In the nursing home we have been limited to ninety days and beyond that the old person may stay on only if boarding and some attendant service, rather than nursing care, are indicated. Recently we have reviewed some sixty cases in nursing homes and have found twenty that should not have been there and have transferred them to hospitals or to private boarding arrangements.

The biggest problem with us, however, is the service called for by old people who are living in their own homes. Of our 55,000 recipients, about one third, or 18,600, live alone: a picture which marks a growing tendency to live alone among people receiving old age assistance in New York City. While that may be perfectly natural and proper for many at sixty-five, it becomes increasingly unsatisfactory as the shadows of life lengthen.

There is, of course, a larger number, 36,400, who live with relatives and friends; many of these, however, are living only with a wife or a husband who is also elderly. We tend to worry less about these, because there is someone to share the responsibility and to report changes to us.

Ill health and impairment present a common crossroad toward the end of life's highway. We provide WPA housekeepers and doctors from the Department for 500 cases of enfeeblement requiring attention. Regular medical visits to chronics are authorized in 1,716 instances for periods of at least 10 weeks. Another group of 1,713 maintained fairly regularly each month get occasional medical attention for acute illnesses. The balance or 51,000 old people, which is a rough figure, are presumably ambulatory and pretty well. We know that many of these attend clinics. In a period of one month we pay for medication at voluntary hospital clinics for 1,153. Special diets causing an increase in food beyond our usual estimate are authorized for 284 on an average each month. We now carry nearly 1,900 such allowances.

I have always hoped that there might be special facilities in this city for the aged in need of psychiatric services, where a good medical tie-up would be offered and a comprehensive type of service would include attention to borderline psychotics. Today only a small number of old people may utilize psychiatric clinics and that on a limited basis.

In a month we average 1,300 movings for our 55,000 people. Some move because of family plans, many because of restlessness, and many others have to move because of vacate orders. We see a steady improvement in housing and so alarming an increase in the rents that we have recently issued an instruction to all recipients that increases in rent must not be contracted for without our approval. Nothing pleases us like getting our people into the public housing projects where rent is reasonable and accommodations are of the most modern kind, however modest as to size.

A busy life for people up to the end—no matter how restricted that life may be so long as it is not self-centered—this is of the greatest importance. I get fresh evidence of its value from letters and leaflets which old friends who are homebound direct to me and from their pleasure at receiving responses to these messages. Even an appointment at an office may be the means of lifting one day above the other and a widening of the horizon for those we all know. We are hopeful that through the pleasant contacts established by means of friendly visitors, a few of our people enrich their lives and bring satisfactions to the volunteers. It is this adequacy of living which we all desire to help tolerably well old people achieve.

In a big division like that of OAA, each staff worker has so many tasks to keep up with—their new and old assignments average 125 old people apiece—that we do not maintain a vital relationship with recipients and look, therefore, to facilities in the community to which the old person can be referred for such helpful contacts. Old age is a lonely, shrinking, inward time at best, and we find our workers turned to repeatedly by their clients as desperate periods come on.

How progressively impoverished their lives are so far as social contacts are concerned is shown all too plainly. Agencies such as church, settlements, and volunteer associations could well emphasize the need for plans for the strengthening of ties for our old population.

It may seem that I have concentrated on the practical problems we meet as a public agency. However, we are well aware that there are infinitely more subtle problems bound up in relationships and attitudes which often elude us on our infrequent visits; some of these we recognize and attack with good, bad, or indifferent success. The limitations in our relief policies bring serious problems of adjustment to those clients accustomed to niceties of living, but on the whole, older people are less demanding in their financial requirements than younger ones. When it is too painful a problem, we suggest their considering referral to a private agency or to an institution which maintains a congenial atmosphere. I sometimes feel like a construction carpenter laying foundation and two by fours when circumstances also call for cabinet makers!

We find, on the whole, that living in family groups is a more natural role for the older person, one changing with the lessening of physical vigor, but here too there is a vast area in which to practice case work had we the delicate skill to interpret the older person to the young members of the family and these to the old age recipient. By and large, we do not traverse this region of relationship practice except in the more obvious areas of service or information as requested.

Mental problems call for these skills, and here we turn to doctors and other community facilities to assist us. I would look to the private agencies to lead the way in this area. We do not require that the present living combination be continued and we encourage visits and experiments in variations of living by permitting the old person vacation trips to children or friends in other parts of the state. This is as far as we can go at present.

OLD AGE, FIRST PERSON SINGULAR *

By George Lawton

WHEN THOSE INTERESTED in the care of the aged gather, there often is one vacant chair at the conference table. Absent is the individual about whom all are talking, the very one all want to make happy—the old person himself. It is *Hamlet* without Hamlet.

Instead of keeping the senescent a ghost at his own memorial sessions, an attempt will be made in what follows to present him in the first person singular. Let us throw on a screen, as it were, a number of these real older people and exhibit a miscellany of their problems in family and institutional living just as *they* see them.

The first is Mrs. Knight:

I am seventy-two years old and have been married since the age of twenty-five. My husband, with whom I have had a happy and active home life, died recently. I have always been around other people and used to be busy in church and school affairs. I have also been pretty independent and have enjoyed the company of young people. A good many of my own friends have died and I am not accustomed to the loneliness which I now have. I am seriously thinking of going to an old age home.

However, unlike some persons of my age and in my situation, I look upon this change as an opportunity to increase my friendships. I realize that homes, like people, must be different. I should therefore like to know a little about the home to which I am going. I should like to meet beforehand a few of the guests and have an opportunity to visit with them. I should like to know what kinds of rules and regulations the

* This chapter represents a weaving together of material brought up in the discussion periods of many of the sessions, particularly meeting No. 9, "Old Age at the Crossroads: Patterns of Living in an Institution." In addition, the author has amplified some of his remarks which had to be summarized during the meetings.

home has. For example, would I be permitted to leave the home for visits? Could I join my friends in Miami in the winter, if circumstances permitted?

If Mrs. Knight has lived the life she just described it should not be hard for her to adjust herself to any modern home for the aged. I can think of several who would be glad to invite her to join them, one in particular being the John Doe Memorial Home.

At the John Doe Home the superintendent would show Mrs. Knight around, introduce her to some of the people, invite her to the library, and have her spend an hour or so in the occupational therapy class. If Mrs. Knight would like to try working on a loom, she might even do that. The Home has a large group of several hundred people, and while there may be some individuals that are not liked by any particular member, Mrs. Knight could choose from among the others those with whom she wants to be friendly.

Unfortunately, the John Doe Home cannot offer her a room for herself. She may have to share it with one or two other people. Every attempt would be made to find roommates with a similar background so that Mrs. Knight would not mind living with them.

I'm reminded of a certain old age home where it became necessary for a Mrs. Breen who had lived alone to give up her privacy and double up with another woman. Mrs. Breen protested that she had never lived alone with another woman. She had been married for fifty years and knew how to get along with a man. If she were placed with a member of the opposite sex she could adjust to that. She understands men. But as for a woman—!

Mrs. Breen lived in a home whose superintendent was himself seventy, and though she could not evade the fate of moving in with another woman, at least she was able to speak her mind and share the poignant irony of the situation with a superintendent who was sympathetic and who did try valiantly to give her a temperamentally congenial roommate.

To return to Mrs. Knight, one might point out that at the John Doe Memorial Home she would be permitted to go out whenever she liked. However, she would be asked to act as if she still were in a family group. Should she go out in the morning, she would be expected to leave word where she was going and when she expected to return. If any member of the Home receives an invitation to visit for a few weeks a friend or relative in Florida or elsewhere, the administration will gladly give its approval for the trip. The member who would like a few weeks' vacation in the summer can have that without any difficulty. The John Doe Home tries to make all of its members as comfortable as possible. It sincerely believes that institutional living offers the aged adequate opportunities for work, recreation, and enjoyment of life as well as for developing satisfying social relationships.

Mrs. Knight apparently has some more questions for she has returned to the screen:

As I said, I always have been very busy—outside my home as well as inside. I wonder if there will be things to do around this John Doe Home so that I can feel I am a part of it. Also, I understand that the Home asks members upon admission to will their property to it. There is a little bequest that I expect to receive. Do I have to sign that over too? If so, where am I going to get the spending money I've always had? Having had control of my own money my entire life, I would not relish being told the things I may or may not do with it!

Mrs. Knight's desire to remain active is very common (though not universal.) Since she has been a housewife, she might be asked to help in the morning for a half hour, possibly to assist in the preparation of the vegetables or she might be asked to come into the laundry, sort sheets, make beds, mend socks, etc. She will have to keep her own room and closet tidy.

In the home there might be another resident who enjoys outside excursions a great deal but is afraid to go out alone. Perhaps Mrs. Knight would like to accompany this member on her walks. As for abandoning her former church or its activities, this is not necessary. She may keep up her previous affiliations, or join a religious group in the home—just as she pleases.

The financial question Mrs. Knight raises is a thorny one. Some homes allow anyone to have access to his own money with the understanding that the funds left after death revert to the home.

In the John Doe Home and a number of others, the resident is permitted to have his own spending money, to buy his own clothes, and to preserve as much of his own preadmission independence as he possibly can.

The next witness, Mrs. Stewart, being duly sworn, deposes:

> My family think I am old and that it is enough for me to just sit where I am put. But it is unbearable for me to do nothing. I don't want to live in an institution but my family won't let me do any work. I am not helpless. I can do certain things and earn my living if given a chance. I have some educational background and have been manager of a house. Is there any place where I can go to find advice and an opportunity to explore my abilities? Why can't there be guidance clinics where old people are treated on the same principles as young children and given the same complete analysis?

Mrs. Stewart may be surprised to learn that the first Old Age Counselling Center was opened by Dr. Lillien J. Martin about twenty years ago in San Francisco. In September, 1943, the writer plans to establish a similar and affiliated center in New York. Nowadays we know a good deal about techniques for restoring an earlier level of mental efficiency and social-emotional functioning to a person in whom a decline has occurred. Within our lifetime, such old age guidance centers will be common throughout the country.

When people reach sixty, they should have a chance to go somewhere for a stock-taking of their abilities and resources: intellectual, social, emotional, and recreational. In our later years, we all want to know what losses we have undergone and what gains we have made. Objective findings showing how we compare with our contemporaries, with young people today, with our youthful self are essential if we are to realize any kind of a vocational and avocational plan adapted to the needs of our older self.

The old person who presents himself at such a guidance bureau is studied to discover his actual and possible interests. This appraisal may or may not lead to paid reëmployment. Even where there is little hope of the latter, if an older person can regain the ability or the *will* to engage in some activity which brings attention, appreciation, or reciprocal services from others or which gives him a sense of worth-while achievement within himself, his remaining years of life may be said to have been salvaged.

In the future colleges and schools of social work will offer courses in the psychological problems of older people and of methods to deal with these problems. And just as educational and penal institutions, hospitals, business concerns, and other organizations have psychologists on their staffs, so every old age home will make definite provisions for some type of psychological service, even though it is a plan in which several homes must share. Such care is fully as necessary as the medical and psychiatric, though the need is not always so obvious. The psychological department can aid in a program of selective admittance, by determining which applicants are suitable to the demands of group living as found in a particular home; it can promote the adjustment of individuals to institutional life and particularly to other individuals in a home, especially in the weeks following admission; it can deal with "problem" senescents and aid in placement outside the home when necessary.

These psychological services would be directed not only to extreme pathological types who are on the verge of requiring custodial care, but to those who have minor types of maladjustments. Even the seemingly well-adjusted can benefit by opportunities for discussion with a psychologist.

In an old age home the members, the administrative board, and the staff all have a need of gerontological psychologists, for reasons of efficiency as well as humaneness.

The staff generally does not have the training or experience which will help them to understand the psychological mechanisms responsible for the behavior of their charges. Since the superintendent and the employees of the home have to take positive administrative and disciplinary action toward their residents, it is not easy to achieve an objective attitude.

The staff most often welcomes a detached view of what is happening, both for its own sake and for that of the residents. Many patterns of behavior and emotional reaction on the part of men and women in the old age home are not likely to change. Moreover, frequently the complaints of older people have little foundation. There is grumbling about the food, complaints about the way rooms are cleaned, allegations about favoritism shown to one resident. While sometimes these complaints may have a basis, often the complaint is psychologically motivated. The old person is complaining not about details of his immediate environment or the administration of the home but about the way life has treated him.

When we consider the psychology of old age, we begin to see that the protests are against the diminished sense of importance, the limitation of activities, the fear of incapacitating infirmity, the loss of attention and love, and not against matters of household routine in themselves. Complaints about food are common because eating and physiological functions in general have become matters of tremendous concern. The world of older persons, as far as intellectual interest and emotional stimulation go, becomes greatly constricted. Food is important as a subject of conversation as well as being a source of nourishment. Moreover, survival seems to depend largely on proper food and medical care. Finally, older people will use for purposes of attention-getting and of asserting their individuality any area—the diningroom and household routine, for example—that brings them into close contact with the administration.

Of course, from time to time there may exist valid causes for complaint. However, the administrator interested in sifting the valid complaints from the purely subjective ones, can make his task easier by utilizing the insights into personality types which the psychologist makes available. The subjective complainers, in fact, need sympathetic help as much, or even more than, the other types. Employees, however, react to the complaints as such, and often make strenuous efforts to rectify the situation without any success, whereupon they have a sense of futility and are filled with self-recrimination. Hence, the staff and administration needs someone to alleviate their sense of guilt. The psychologist is useful in helping institutional personnel to accept casually certain senescent reactions, at the same time sensitizing it to those fundamental needs of the aged which they might otherwise overlook.

The screen which has shown no new actor for some time now reflects the image of Mrs. Fenton, whose turn it is to air what is on her mind:

I have been in a home for seven years, turning over $300 to it when I entered. I have an income of $21 a month. For the last four years I have been dissatisfied there and would like to get out and try rooming again. Suppose I went out on my own will and discovered it was a mistake. You see, I have goiter and it might not be easy to get along by myself. Would the home take me back without any hard feeling?

There is no need to tell Mrs. Fenton that $21 a month is not very much to live on or that her physical condition makes living alone quite a gamble. However, old people are not children whose behavior and personal regimen we must direct. All we can do is to sit down and talk the problem over with her. Any decision arrived at is the personal responsibility of Mrs. Fenton—and no one else.

Every old age home has examples of individuals who have been members for a long time but whose dissatisfaction or maladjustment increases with the years. In some of these cases it seems advisable that such a person live on the outside. In one case, where there was no life contract, a woman left with her husband in a quarrel over finances. They had inherited a considerable sum of money and refused to consent to an arrangement whereby part of the inheritance would be made available to other members of the home, while control of the rest would remain with the old couple. The husband died and his widow tried living alone, first with her children and then with relatives. These arrangements failed to satisfy her, and in much chastened mood she tentatively took up with the home the matter of readmission on its own terms. Though when this woman left she was angry and indignant and the administration was very annoyed, she was accepted without any recriminations or reprisals, and soon returned to her former role of active and happy leadership.

No home has a fixed policy about readmissions. If a person asks to be taken back, the situation is considered on its merits. The best interests of the individual and of other members are compared and in this way a decision is reached.

Another figure is looming up before us. This time, for a change, it is male:

My name is Carrington, I'm sixty-nine and live in the Richard Roe Home. I had a roommate whose eyes were pretty bad—he was eighty, but full of go. Several times he had narrow escapes and minor injuries but still he insisted on crossing the streets between corners. Finally he was severely injured, lived on in pain for three years, and died. After the accident, the police captain sent for the head of our home, Mrs. Andrews, and scolded her very severely for shirking her responsibilities. He felt it was her duty to have forcibly kept my roommate off the streets and implied that she had practically committed murder.

Mrs. Andrews was a kind person, always eager to do the right thing. In fact, she once remarked to me, "I've never been quite the same since that officer spoke to me." However much Mrs. Andrews smiled as she said this, you could see it bothered her. I myself don't find that she was at fault or know what else could have been done. Anyway, my roommate went at a ripe age.

Mr. Carrington brings up quite a problem. Of course, we cannot allow a person to walk off a precipice. It is truly dangerous for the older person to "live dangerously" and it may be even more risky for those to whose care the old person has been entrusted. A simple practical situation will illustrate the difficulty of arriving at a decision which will do neither the aged person nor his group an injustice. What, for example, should the superintendent of an old age home do with men who smoke in bed? He could prohibit smoking in bed on the threat of dismissal from the home. He could look the other way and simply pay the cost of damage, seeing to it in the meantime that his fire fighting equipment was of the best. Finally he could try to understand the causes for this smoking and secure the individual's coöperation in refraining.

There is a tendency for people to resume childish habits in old age or rather to release the reins on impulses that had never disappeared but which were held in check by fear of social disapproval or punishment.

Smoking is an important source of relaxation, especially smoking in bed, since the latter is in a way a reliving of the situation that existed when the baby was soothed by the mother's breast or by the bottle. The superintendent could try to provide activities which will help lessen the need for such an "infantile regression" as smoking in bed. Occupational and recreational therapy would be useful and a general psychological rehabilitation might be necessary.

Probably the simplest solution is to have a smoking room where all the men might repair for a short or long smoking session just before bedtime. Moral pressure could be exerted by the members of the men's smoking club upon one another by having as the club's first rule that no one could remain a member in good standing who smoked again after he left the clubroom each night.

As a general principle, however, I favor letting the old person live and die in the manner which suits him best, assuming he is mentally and physically able to carry such responsibility, and assuming he does not place the group in jeopardy by his actions. If you have one hundred old people and allow them a good deal of discretion as to how they dispose of their powers, in the long run you will be conferring more benefits than if you deny them such freedom of choice.

The great problem in dealing with older men and women is to give them some outlet for their aggressive and pleasure-seeking tendencies. In most families containing an older person such an outlet is unavailable. When the older person comes to live with his children, the family tends to shelter him just as the old age home would. However, the old person, instead of being relieved of all responsibility, should be given some of the necessary jobs in the household.

There is the Webster family for example. Mr. and Mrs. Webster both worked, but she was on a leave of absence from her position because of a baby that had just arrived. About this time, her father came to live with them. There was plenty of room, but the old man was unhappy. Then Mrs. Webster returned to work. Although there were servants in the home to take care of the baby, the grandfather took over certain tasks and developed a particular sense of responsibility toward the child. From that time on, he became much happier and far less a source of friction. Of course such participation in family life of a grandparent is useful unless it exceeds certain limits. Unfortunately, in our society the limits for such participation are soon reached.

However, occasionally an old person will seek responsibility and be perfectly willing to take on a particular task; then when the latter becomes too arduous, he is filled with resentment at his own inadequacy, but vents his feelings on others. Such an individual is like a child who tends to overstep the limits of his abilities, partly out of anxiety to justify his importance, partly out of enthusiasm. Then he rapidly tires and becomes vexed. Anyone dealing with old people must constantly try to achieve a balance between what the old person can do and what he wants to do.

Individual differences are present in senescence even more than in childhood. It takes a lifetime of experience to develop all the variations in human behavior. Yet our first impulse is to think of old people as *old* people. They are not that. They are old *people:* men and women of such and such an age. If one has to choose between overtaxing or undertaxing the older individual, it is better, in my opinion, to make a mistake in the overtaxing direction. Such a "mistake" in judgment is based on the two principles that we seldom use all our resources, least of all in old age, and that an emotionally healthy person appraises situations with realistic correctness and hence is unlikely to overtax himself.

Social engineers need to invent outlets for old people, that is, need to make available tasks, duties, "roles"—as Lawrence K. Frank puts it in his paper—which will allow older people a chance to assert themselves. The aged should be used in the community, preferably with pay: if not, then on a volunteer basis. But they should be used. There are many essential services of which older people are capable, once we accept them as first-class citizens who are to be evaluated in terms of their ability to do a particular task.

The next oldster to be made articulate raises a question that severely tests our feelings about the relative value of the younger and older generations. Here is Mrs. Park, aged seventy-two, who steps forward to say:

I am living with my daughter and her children. Money is scarce. What is to be done when a choice has to be made between the younger and older generation? While I think young people should be given the preference, sometimes we have to weigh medical treatment for an aged individual, which may be a life and death matter, over against a college education or professional school for the boy or girl.

Mrs. Park herself realizes that potentialities exist for the young and for the old. On the side of young people is the fact that we must help them in every way prepare for the problems they will meet in later years. On the other hand, the older person represents an investment of a great many years and we should allow this investment to bear interest as long as possible.

It often happens that we allow our loyalties to the older generation to involve us in difficult situations. Some children find the relationship to their parents burdensome, either because of their own emotional dependence on the old people, or because of the latter's financial or emotional dependence on them. To compensate for this hostile feeling, the child develops a tremendous sense of guilt which shows itself in excessive fear of neglecting the parents' financial or physical welfare. The child may pay for this sense of guilt by taking care of his parents in a way which does economic and psychological damage to himself and his mate. This may not be so bad, but it is serious when the damage is done to the grandchildren; an excellent example of such a case is given by Miss Randall in her paper. No adult should transfer to his children the consequences of his sense of guilt toward his parents.

The solution, I believe, is to narrow the range of choice between the older and younger generation. Both have claims on our time, our sympathies, our energies, and our pocketbooks. We should encourage coöperation between the generations, instead of competition. But whenever there is a conflict of claims, it should be the younger generation that gets the preference.

Our imaginary screen is darkened by the figure of a man for a second time. He states:

I am seventy-four and living in a home. On the same floor there is a lady with whom I am friendly. We would like to marry, even though we are both quite old—she also is in the seventies. The home will not consent to this. The best it can do is to arrange that my friend and I should be buried in the same grave. We must be satisfied to be together in death if we can't be in life.

In the same home with me there is a man and woman who have been so devoted to each other for sixteen years that the old lady now forgets and speaks to her friend in public by endearing first names and he does likewise. It seems very unfair and even silly for the home to forbid marriages between residents. Even if my friend and I had the smallest of rooms together, it would be better than what we now have.

In one home the writer knows, a man of seventy-four married, the marriage lasting less than a year. The man, who had been married twice before, said that the happiest time of his life had been spent in that third marriage. In another old age home two members, very advanced in years, married. Both had families by previous marriages. Husband and wife said that their last years of married life were very happy for the simple reason that, as they said, their own families had given them up and they had been sent to the City Home. The old couple felt that the companionship they enjoyed gave them a great advantage over the other residents.

In another case at the City Home a man and woman wanted to marry, but because the woman was feeble-minded the advisability of a union was seriously questioned. However, the couple was finally married, and exchanged the home for old age assistance and home relief. Three years later they were doing exceptionally well and were very happy. At a recent Christmas they put on quite a celebration for friends of theirs still at the home.

Another marriage at the City Home which was questioned was that of a man who wanted to marry a wheel-chair patient at the Chronic Disease Hospital on Welfare Island, New York. It was decided finally that if they wanted to marry there could be no real objection to their union. The man and woman took a chance and are getting along very well in the three-room apartment that is now their home. He is very tender and considerate and they are extremely happy. Who is the ultimate judge to decide whether this old pair should have married or not? The only test is the happiness of a couple and the ability they have to get along with each other.

When we think of eligibility for marriage we have in mind the physical and mental health of possible children and many other factors that apply only in marriages of young people. However, the ordinary objections to a feeble-minded or invalid mate do not hold in the case of old people. An old lover and his lass do not have to consider the health or happiness of offspring. They have only each other to look after and think of. Dr. Lewellys F. Barker tells of a very amusing experience in connection with this matter of marriage in old age:

In June, 1927, a wealthy man of international eminence asked if he could have a private professional interview with me with regard to a personal matter that concerned him deeply. I arranged for him to lunch with me in a small room at the club where he told me his story. Born in 1850, he had had a happy and a very successful career except that he had not been able to marry the woman that he loved. She was 22 years younger than he, and when she was 27 years of age he had asked her to marry him and she had accepted, as she loved him devotedly. Because he was so many years her senior and had dandled her as a little girl upon his knee, he felt compunctions about marrying her and felt that he must break the engagement. On two occasions later, he renewed the invitation to marriage, was accepted, but broke off the engagements quickly because of some psychic obstacle. Though able to engage decisively in large financial matters, he seemed unable to meet the particular new situation of getting married. Their wary friendship continued. When near this woman he showed such devotion that she thought that since he could not bring himself to the point of marrying her it would be less embarrassing for her to live in Europe, so as to see him only occasionally when she revisited America.

Though the patient had had a serious heart attack in 1926 he felt better again and he told me that he had come to the conclusion that he must marry the woman of his choice in the hope of having at least a few years of relatively good health and loving companionship. After hearing his story I told him that before giving my consent from the medical side I must first have an interview with the lady concerned and this was arranged for two days later (on Sunday,) when he brought her to my house and I had a long frank talk with her alone. The whole matter was thoroughly ventilated and I learned that she had continued to love this man for over 25 years and was perfectly willing to marry him, though she felt sure from previous experience that he could not possibly bring himself to the point of marriage. She said that since his interview with me two days earlier he had spent two sleepless nights and that she was convinced that the same peculiar psychic condition that had prevented his marriage on three earlier occasions was again developing in him! I told her of the heart attack he had had and of the possibilities of serious illness during the few years he might have ahead of him and asked her if, visualizing all the circumstances, she would still be willing to marry him if I could arrange for it. She said that she would, especially because of his present feeling of urgent need for her companionship and aid: she felt sure, however, that neither I nor anybody else could really get him to marry. I then saw the two of them together and asked him if he still felt as he did two days earlier. He replied that he did but that the only objection to the marriage was his fear that he might become a burden upon, and be harmful to, the woman he loved. Excusing myself from them for a few moments I found out by telephone how to get a marriage license on Sunday, got the consent of the Rev. Dr. Kinsolving "to marry two people who were at the time in my office and who should by all means be married at once" and then called a taxi. I asked them to go into town with me. The patient immediately asked, "What does this mean?" I told him that I was taking them into the city to be married. He immediately protested, said it was impossible, and that he must have a certain time to prepare. My reply was that he had had some 27 years to prepare and hadn't yet got ready; this time, I had made the preparations and I was going to see to it that they were married that afternoon. We secured the license, Dr. Kinsolving married them, and his daughter and I witnessed the marriage! The patient lived until mid November, 1932, dying at the age of 82. It is interesting that the symptoms of disease of his heart passed off after his marriage in a remarkable way. He and his wife had 5½ years of happiness and increasing contentment that they would have missed entirely if that psychasthenic "quirk" of the man had not been handled clinically in the right way. I was much gratified when his wife wrote me on the second anniversary of their marriage: "I wonder if any two human beings have ever owed another as much as we owe you." *

Of course, there are many older people who do not wish to take advantage of opportunities to marry. The writer was once talking to a widow in her middle seventies about an eighty-one-year-old friend of hers whom she could have married had she so desired. She remarked: "While I like him and enjoy his company, I also

* Quoted from *Problems of Ageing*, edited by E. V. Cowdry, 2d ed. revised. (Baltimore, Williams and Wilkins, 1942), pp. 850–52.

value my privacy. After a lifetime of considering one man's wishes, I want to be alone and take care of myself. My friend is only a few doors away from me in this home, and I see as much of him as if we were married. We spend hours together, take walks, eat at the same table, and go to the movies. The sexual relationship is not a factor for us any longer, so we both feel there is nothing that marriage can offer which we do not already have."

Suppose we now turn our attention to marriages in which not both but only one of the partners is old. What then? We know that most December and May unions are notoriously foredoomed to failure. Yet we must keep an open mind here, because occasionally such a marriage does succeed.

Mr. George Bruce at sixty-four had been a widower three years when he married a girl of twenty-one. All his relatives thought the marriage would go to smash. Surprisingly, in a little over a year a son was born; ten years later, when Mr. Bruce was seventy-five, a daughter came.

Both children were very brilliant, winning scholarships to leading universities. The boy became an engineer and the woman a musician. One of Mr. Bruce's granddaughters, interestingly enough, went into the field of old age care. The marriage lasted until Mr. Bruce was ninety, and he and his wife were completely happy throughout those years. The products of such an unpromising marriage were two splendid, talented children. It is true the wife was left a widow at forty-eight, a relatively young age, but she does not feel at all cheated by life. In fact, Mrs. Bruce is sure that she had driven a rather good bargain with it.

Next on the invisible stage are an old couple, with the husband acting as spokesman:

We've just returned to New York City after having been away in a small village for several years. We were very unhappy there and couldn't wait until we got back to where we have lived all our lives. We're not so well off here as we were in the small village, and our children think we were foolish to return. Yet we are like many friends our age who would not accept an old age home in another state because, as they say, "We do not want to go that far and be completely away from our friends."

This old couple bring up a very challenging problem. Is growing old a happier process in a rural rather than a city environment? Some persons believe that country life allows older people more scope for enriched experiences than does the city. The writer is himself city bred and apt, therefore, to sentimentalize about the country, as well as to feel that the village or small town offers certain facilities for living that would make the later years more complete. There are older persons who have lived in the city for many years and then have gone to the country, which they would never leave afterward—Mr. Malcolm Strait, for example. He was known as the "Beau Brummel of New York," for he was a leader in setting styles for men. Marrying for a second time in his later years, he moved to a tiny village in upper New York State, where he is happier than he has ever been in the metropolis in which he had been born and reared.

Those who have observed old people in small communities cannot say that they are happier than old people in cities, but they do feel that rural old age is free of some of the complications that accompany life in the highly urban center.

It is not so much a question of whether we are to vote for old age in a suburban rather than a urban locality, as it is an individual problem in overcoming background inertia: can Mr., Miss, or Mrs. X., who has lived in a highly urban center adjust to a rural or semi-suburban environment, and vice versa? As we grow older we have less ability to change our style of living, thinking, and feeling than do most young people. The senescent as a rule wants the pattern of life to which he has been accustomed in the past. He is reluctant to make a transfer from a known situation or environment to an unknown one and generally finds it very hard to make the adaptations required when he goes to a new locality, though young persons make this adjustment with relative ease all the time.

This reluctance in old age to accept alterations in routine and locale is one possible objection to "Southern Villages" as described by Lawrence K. Frank, where large numbers of older people could be accommodated comfortably through efficient use of living facilities. Many people would refuse to pay the price of giving up all the ties they have accumulated in a lifetime in order to participate in a village plan far away from their home, neighborhood, friends, and churches. Leaving one's home town on a visit is vastly different from giving it up permanently. However, even here we can't be too dogmatic, for warm climates like that of Florida and California, combined with inexpensive living arrangements, are apt to have so strong an attraction for older people on pensions that it offsets the pain of adapting oneself to unfamiliar surroundings.

The first and most famous colony for the aged in the United States was established at Millville, New Jersey, in 1937. There are said to be similar villages abroad, usually under the auspices of the church. The colony at Millville, called Roosevelt Park, draws on the old people in and near Millville itself. Incidentally, the writer, having made a close study of the Millville plan, believes that it is one of the best solutions of the problem of finding inexpensive ways to give dependent and physically able old people a sense of independence.* A group of twenty or so old men and women, with an average age of seventy-seven or seventy-eight, take care of themselves, cooking and cleaning in three-room cottages for which they pay $4.00 a month rent.

There are many different solutions, however, to the problems of older people—all equally good, depending on the individual for whom the solution is intended. Miss Ruth Hill, for example, is the proponent of a public housing program, especially one in which whole blocks of apartments may be set aside for aged persons. The fifty apartments of this sort in the Fort Greene Houses, Brooklyn, New York, may be said to represent a step in the right direction. Miss Hill feels that older people who live inside a city or town are better off than those on the outskirts, because they have access to many services, particularly medical, and that the particular drawback to the Millville idea is in caring for those who become ill. Actually, however, the sickness problem is a minor one at Roosevelt Park. The health of those who are able and willing to live in their own cottages and take care of all their own needs is good to begin with. Moreover, a visiting physician is on call whenever needed. In

* See "Not Quite Heaven," *Saturday Evening Post*, May 9, 1942.

case of illness requiring hospitalization, the patient can be removed to the village hospital two miles or so away.

The entire question of institutional versus noninstitutional arrangements, of independent living in one's own home versus boarding out, depends on what the individual wants, assuming that financial and medical aspects of the case allow flexibility of choice. Some men and women enjoy being in the midst of a large group of people. A next type wants to be close to fellow beings but not too close, seeking to be among people without belonging to them. Such persons adapt easily to a large group and even enjoy it, though remaining on the outside. Others want to give themselves and be absorbed in turn and crave intimate life in small family units. They can endure large "families" only by forming cliques. A final social type desires contact with people only occasionally. The rest of the time he wants to be left severely alone. Isolation suits him best.

It follows that if one could remove the institutional stigma from old age homes, many old people would be happier there than in a private domicile. A group arrangement can often take care of our material and physical needs better than can private and individual planning.

While on the subject of institutional arrangements for the aged, the writer must give voice to a strong conviction of his. A certain number of old people, while technically psychotic, if we are considering only mental processes, are actually no danger to themselves or others, and the care they require is of a medical or nursing variety rather than custodial or psychiatric. Such men and women do not belong in a mental hospital or need the services of such institutions. It is the writer's judgment that there is a great deal of overlapping among patients in the undisturbed wards of state hospitals; cases in such an institution as the Chronic Disease Hospital on Welfare Island, New York City; and patients in the infirmary of the City Home, also on Welfare Island.

Every large community requires several hospitals for older people whose chief need is medical and nursing care. In this group might come patients now designated as psychotic according to the rules of the American Psychiatric Association, and therefore to be treated only in a "mental" hospital. If a layman may enter where angels fear to tread, the writer offers the hope that one of these years the Association will change its classification of mental diseases to keep pace with the practical consequences of a rapidly aging population.

Dr. John H. Travis, Superintendent of Manhattan State Hospital, Ward's Island, New York, has been kind enough to furnish the editor with a statement very much to the point here. Dr. Travis writes:

> It is my opinion, based on my own day-to-day contacts, that the commitment of seniles and arteriosclerotics is not being handled as efficiently as it might be both from the view of the individual patient and of society.
>
> For one thing, too many seniles and arteriosclerotics are being committed to our state institutions. A considerable percentage of both groups could and should be cared for by their own families or by the city or county in institutions other than mental hospitals.
>
> Commitments, moreover, are too precipitate. Old people belonging to the groups described should, before hospitalization, be kept under observation for longer periods than is now customary. In many instances old people are rushed to state institutions when the basic problem is a relatively simple physical condition which has thrown the individual temporarily off balance. With improvement of this physical condition there is very often an amelioration of the mental symptoms to such a degree that the individuals become tractable and require no more than home care.
>
> One very curious aspect of this entire matter of commitment is a change which has come about in the attitude of people toward state institutions, a change which has both its good and bad features. A generation ago, sons and daughters considered it a disgrace to send their mothers and fathers to "asylums"; now in numerous instances children are only too ready to transfer the responsibility to the state. Afterward when the old person is in an institution and it is found that he will be much better off at home, it is very difficult to induce his family to take him back.
>
> Still another difficulty which comes up today in connection with the commitment of seniles and arteriosclerotics is that many come to a state hospital on the verge of a moribund condition. There were 309 deaths of patients with these psychoses during the first four months

of 1943; 31, or 10 percent, died within the first week following admission and 143, or 46 percent, died within the first month.

As far as society's stake goes, the cost of caring for the seniles and arteriosclerotics is too high. They are housed in buildings of expensive construction, whereas simpler structures erected by the city or county would suffice. What is even more regrettable is that these cases are committed in such large numbers that they cause a bottleneck whereby the younger patients, such as schizophrenics, are prevented from receiving the individual attention they require.*

In the future, the needs of the aged will not depend for satisfaction on one facility. A variety of arrangements will be available to deal with the principal situations in which old people find themselves. These facilities will be geared to take care of the differences (physical, mental, and temperamental) between the old and the young, and between one old person and another.

Frances Perkins has a favorite story which concerns her grandfather. When the latter was ninety-two years old he went to the village shoemaker to have a pair of shoes made. He was very particular about what he wanted and gave detailed instructions to the cobbler. The latter grew a little annoyed and said, "Mr. Perkins, you are a very old man. How long do you expect to live anyway?" Grandfather came back like a flash. "Young man, I want you to know that there are very few people who die at my age."

In the coming decades, there will be more and more people over sixty dying. The necessity of finding ways to meet the varied needs of old people will grow steadily more imperative. We must therefore remember that a new view of childhood gradually developing within the past century ultimately gave rise to real children who knew a happier enriched home and school life because of changed attitudes toward the possibilities of childhood. In the same way, students of old age care who do not easily find examples of a mentally hygienic and a wholly useful and admirable senescence, must invent such a kind of later maturity. Should this happen, the next century may be one of the "maturate," just as the last one was of the child.

* Letter to Editor, May 24, 1943.

HOW IT FEELS TO BE SEVENTY-FIVE AND A WOMAN *

WE OLD PEOPLE have been given a present; it comes wrapped in a rather wrinkled cover. Quite a heavy package it is and not too easy to carry.

The donors are our physicians, dietitians, boards of health—and what have you. The gift is a score or more of years than we were wont to expect.

Having made their presentation, they watch us grow older and are alarmed at the Frankenstein act they have put on. They cry, "What in Heaven's name are we going to do with all these old people? They have to be fed and housed and cared for and the bulk of them are so difficult to get along with!"

So they call in the psychologists to help. The psychologists are supposed to assist us toward a wholesome social metabolism, thus preventing the menace to civilization we already threaten to become.

We used to take it for granted that at sixty we were a finished product, unalterably and beautifully "jelled," but we learn that we are far from finished; so we buckle down to the job of trying to make ourselves as healthy, happy, and useful as possible—with the psychologists to inspire and direct.

I have been by way of knowing intimately a number of old people and find that the sense of fellowship tends to become closer with our years. So I find myself slipping into the editorial "we," for the decade from seventy to eighty seems to me to include a greater number of like characteristics than any other.

We are inclined to be garrulous, and as impatient, combative, sensitive, and irritable as spoiled children. If our inhibitions have

* *Editor's Note:* The writer is nearer eighty than seventy and is spending what she calls, "Some of the very happiest years of my life" in a home for the aged—therefore the anonymity. She was present in the audience at the Welfare Council lectures and greatly enjoyed having the experts diagnose and treat her case. No other auditor was by profession "an old person."

not been built up by wise parents and painful experiences, we are not pleasant to live with. We look backward too much, forward to the immediate future too little, talk too much; listen, read, and think too little, and most of us pray only during an emergency.

Writing of old age is much like describing an illness; a chronic illness never to be cured but which must be endured stoically and cheerfully, with courage and fortitude, and more important still —with humor and *curiosity*. For to be curious is to be interested, with keen desire to learn the how, why, when, and where of every daily happening in national and international events and in characters and personalities. A humorous and alertly interested mind keeps its youth and strength and is stimulating to itself and to others.

Mental and physical inertness we must fight with our whole being. Otherwise, we develop hypochondriasis, the most dreaded of all old age diseases. Alexis Carrel warns us against it time and again. Personally, I confess that it is one of my special devils. It is an insidious foe lying in wait to lull one into an alluring coma of body and spirit.

Young people help us to throw off this kind of indolence, especially our children. They rescue us from so unfortunate a malady, for they are part of our cherished and dearly loved, tenderly protected Old Selves! They are the greatest incentives and pleasures of our lives because we live again in their trials or triumphs. If the second and third generation are not wiser and finer than we, we know we have failed in the most important work of our lives.

If we actually have succeeded in raising other than a "generation of vipers," and have created something along the line of modern human beings to whom we may lift our eyes in a noble kind of envy or admiration, we are in danger of becoming the victims of a slightly cringing pride. Perhaps then they will tell us that we are suffering from an inferiority complex. This may be true. When we are tired of our uninteresting lives and our painful bodies and forgetful brains, our children and children's children awaken in us a new zest for living and prove that fresh and piquant surprises are waiting just around every corner.

I think a cultivated person is likely to be more interested in international and civic affairs when old than when middle-aged because we have more time to think. Middle-aged persons are apt to be confused by the many needs of house, children, and budget. In our enforced idleness, we have more time. And because of past experience, we possess a greater realization of the influence of every individual, whether it be in the mere casting of intelligent votes or in other innumerable activities in which we now at last have leisure to take our part.

A beloved old lady of eighty said to me that old age is like pioneering in a new country because every day something new is learnt about our change in bodies and minds. She said that even if these changes are not pleasant, *she* found them interesting! This is one way of dealing with the loss of hair and complexion, the larger shoes, shoulder humps, caved-in mouths, and general slowing up of mind and body. There certainly is no closing our eyes to these inevitable facts.

But to balance such humiliating discomforts, it is pleasant to know that we care very much less about such things (or do we?). Then, too, there is the balm of realizing we are no longer able to suffer the mental agonies often endured in youth and middle age. Almost nothing can happen after seventy plus to give us the unbearable distresses of mind and spirit that we somehow managed to live through in the past. Perhaps we have developed a harder shell covering our emotions. Perhaps our glands are less active. I *know* we have a better sense of proportion. We know that cruelties and injustices in time lose their strength or, should we be the aggressors, that they may be expatiated by each of us through patient and humble kindnesses to those whom we have offended.

The French have a beautifully true saying, "To understand all, is to forgive all." Understanding begets sympathy, sympathy begets tolerance, kindness, and even love.

The loss of friends and family is bound to deprive us of dearly prized happiness; but there is a palliative in knowing that the earthly span of their troubles is over and that our own growing infirmities have been separating us more and more from enjoying their beloved companionship as had been our wont.

I think in old age we are more easily amused and have a greater gratitude for daily comforts and blessings than younger persons, who are apt to take things for granted. Biologically, we are at ease in our last third of life. Men are our pleasant companions and warm friends, and the tingle of mental stimulation is not lacking. But they are no longer essential nor are they tiresome problems as they often were in youth. Instead we gather closer to our hearts our best loved women friends and find that:

> From first beginnings,
> Out to the undiscovered ends
> There's nothing worth the toil of winning
> But laughter and the love of friends.
>
> (Hilaire Belloc)

The spirit of service for others is perhaps the greatest of the happinesses of elderly persons and one of which many never tire. We find a deep satisfaction, or what Dr. Sadler calls a "sense of elation," in doing for our congeners or for our children the most disagreeable duties. When melancholy threatens to mark us for her own, we shake off the cloud and regain poise and cheerfulness the moment we render a service. It matters not in the least whether the service rendered be great or small.

I spoke of the necessity of shaking off inertia. Quite as important is the need to keep our thoughts in constructive channels, to plan for the happier next thing to do. I have learnt that the habit of going over and over the various occasions upon which I have played the fool in the past is a mental regurgitation prone to afflict sleepless nights and is wholly futile and weakening. I turn on my light, spread a quilt on the floor, and, flat on my back with arms straight at the sides, lift them slowly with a deep slow intake of breath until they rest on the floor above my head. The lungs are filled to capacity, then I lower the arms as slowly with a thorough expulsion of breath. When this has been done twenty or thirty times, the circulation is fully restored. Concentrating on counting, drawing in and expelling of air, and the whole rhythmic action of this exercise clears the brain and tends toward sleep.

We so often do look back over the past even when we are busiest, and face the fact that we have not often made the very best of what we have had. I quote Margaret Wilkinson's poem as expressing best this trend of thought:

I never cut my neighbor's throat,
  My neighbor's gold I never stole;
I never spoiled his house and land,
  But God have mercy on my soul!

For I am haunted night and day,
  By all the deeds I have not done.
O unattempted loveliness!
  O costly valor never won!

and I wonder what loveliness I am letting slip away in these last "here and now" years. It is a thought that brings me up standing. The psychologists tell us that every situation however seemingly narrow holds out to us every possible opportunity for growth, for heroism, for spiritual development.

Imbedded in the inner consciousness of all persons during their last decades, I am sure, is a seeking attitude with respect to higher power. How do we regard what we call God? It is a delicate subject to approach, a difficult confession to put into words.

I believe intensely in a Great Plan toward the development of the spirituality of the human race, recognizing the infinitely slow progress toward this desired and essential accomplishment. My most intelligent prayer I believe to be that I may avoid any thought, word, or deed that may cause the slightest delay toward its fulfillment, that I may be quietly able to advance it in however small a fashion. I believe prayer to be a necessity and recognize the beneficial effects of prayer upon every part of the human body, mind, and spirit. It is an appeal to that great natural law of aspiration, toward a higher, finer development, which we must acknowledge is demonstrated in every form of life from the amoeba up to the complexity of the finest human being.

I do believe that prayer (aspiration) is futile without constant *practical effort* to think and act toward the ends so desired. I believe in keeping our minds wide open and friendly toward every creed and that what the Friends (Quakers) call the "Inner Light" illuminating each soul is that which each must follow.

After seventy or eighty I think few of us greatly dread death. There is a natural shrinking from an unknown future; but here again *curiosity* plays a part; we want very much to know what is going to occur after the familiar *now.*

In *Through the Looking Glass,* the White Queen says, "I will give you something to believe. I am just 101, five months, and a day." "I can't believe that!" said Alice. "Can't you?" the White Queen said in a pitying tone. "Try again. Draw a long breath and shut your eyes." Alice laughed. "There is no use trying," she said. "One *can't* believe in impossible things." "I dare say you haven't had much practice," said the Queen. "When I was your age I always did it for a half-hour a day. Why, sometimes I believed as many as six impossible things before breakfast."

In this modern, up-to-date world where miracles that had always been impossible happen so often, I rather envy the White Queen. For I too must learn each day to put newly discovered natural laws in the place of old myths. So, whether we think there is a future life or not, I insist upon contemplating its possibilities, and wish to keep an open mind because a mental *status quo* is to be dreaded more than any death of the physical body.

That frail, old philosopher-poet Alexander Pope tells us:

> Hope humbly then; on trembling pinions soar.
> Await the great teacher Death, and God adore.

BIBLIOGRAPHY

The following references are intended, partly to document the different chapters in the book, but mostly to offer an idea of the varied approaches to the subject of mental health in old age and to indicate some of the more important contributions in connection with each of these approaches.

"Adventure of Old Age, The" (editorial). *The Family* (Feb., 1938).

Allen, D. E. "Nursing Care of the Aged and Chronically Ill Patient," *Journal of the Indiana Medical Association* (1939), 32: 409–12.

Anderson, R. N. The Disabled Man and His Vocational Adjustment. New York, Institute for the Crippled and Disabled, 1932.

Anderson, Rose G. Some Technological Aspects of Counseling Adult Women. *Journal of Applied Psychology* (1938), 22: 455–569.

Atkin, Samuel. "The Psychoanalytic Point of View," in symposium "Old Age and Aging," *American Journal of Orthopsychiatry* (1940), 10: 79–84.

Babcock, Harriet. "An Experiment in the Measurement of Mental Deterioration," *Archives of Psychology* (1930), 18: No. 117, p. 105.

—— "Personality and Efficiency of Mental Functioning," *American Journal of Orthopsychiatry* (July, 1940), 10: 527–32.

—— "The Level-Efficiency Theory of Intelligence," *Journal of Psychology* (April, 1941).

—— Time and the Mind. Cambridge, Mass., Sci-Art Publishers, 1941.

Barker, L. F. "Ageing from the Point of View of the Clinician," in E. V. Cowdry, *Problems of Ageing,* 2d ed., rev., pp. 832–52.

—— "The Senile Patient," *Annals of Internal Medicine* (1933), 6: 1125–35.

—— "Convalescence of Old Age Patients," *Bulletin of the New York Academy of Medicine* (1940), 16: 105–16.

Barkin, Solomon. "The Employment of the Older Worker; the Economically Middle-Aged." *Journal of the American Statistical Association* (March, 1933, supplement), 27: No. 177-A, pp. 102–8.

Becker, S. W. "Treatment of the Skin in the Aged," *Medical Clinics of North America* (1940), 24: 139.

Bennett, S. Old Age; Its Cause and Prevention; the Story of an Old Body and Face Made Young. New York, Dodd, Mead, 1912.

Blai, Boris. "It's in Your Hands," *American Magazine* (1940), 129: 51–53.

Bloodworth, Jessie A. Social Consequences of Prolonged Unemployment. Minneapolis, University of Minnesota Press, 1933. University of Minnesota Employment Stabilization Research Institute, Vol. 2, No. 5.

Boas, Ernest P. The Unseen Plague; Chronic Illness. New York, J. J. Augustin, 1940.

Boggs, T. R. "Some Therapeutic Problems of Old Age," *Virginia Medical Monthly* (1924–25), 51: 270–73.

Bond, C. (pseud. of O. Conner). "Age, the Great Adventure," *Hygeia* (1940), 18: 14–16.

Boynton, Paul L. "Relationship of Intelligence to Age," in article on "Intelligence and Intelligence Tests," *Encyclopedia of Educational Research* (1941), pp. 627–29.

Britten, R. H. "Sex Differences in Physical Impairment in Adult Life," *American Journal of Hygiene* (1931), 13: 741–70.

Brody, M. B. "A Survey of the Results of Intelligence Tests in Psychosis," *British Journal of Medical Psychology* (1942), 19: Pt. 2, pp. 215–61.

Brooks, B. "Surgery in Patients of Advanced Age," *Annals of Surgery* (1937), 105: 481–95.

Brookes, T. P., and F. H. Everhardt. "Fractured Hips in Aged; Improved Prognosis through Physical Therapy," *Archives of Physical Therapy* (1939), 20: 29–34.

Browning, Grace. "Social Service and the Aged," *The Family* (Dec., 1936).

Brown, C. F. G., and R. E. Dolkart. "General Remarks on Care of Aged," *Medical Clinics of North America* (1940), 24: 3–8.

Brown, Ralph. "Effect of Age on the Speed-Power Relationship, with Reference to Tests of Intelligence." *Journal of Educational Psychology* (Sept., 1938), 29: 413–18.

Brunie, L. J. "Geriatrics; Contribution of 25 Carefully Studied Patients Who Are Active and in Good Health beyond 80 Years of Age," *California and Western Medicine* (1938), 49: 369–72.

Brunot, Holmes, and Whitacre. "Individualized Services for the Aged." New York, Family Welfare Association of America, 1941.

Bryan, Alice I. "Can There Be a Science of Bibliotherapy?" *Library Journal* (1939), 64: 773–76.

—— "Personality Adjustment through Reading," *Library Journal* (1939), 64: 573–76.

—— "The Psychology of the Reader," *Library Journal* (1939), 64: 7–12.

Bühler, Charlotte. Der menschliche Lebenslauf als psychologisches Problem. Leipzig, Hirzel, 1933.

—— "The Curve of Life as Studied in Biography," *Journal of Applied Psychology* (1935), 19: 404–9.

Calkins, E. E. Care and Feeding of Hobby Horses. New York, Leisure League of America, 1934.

Cameron, Norman. "A Study of Thinking in Senile Deterioration and Schizophrenic Disorganization," *American Journal of Psychology* (Oct., 1938), 51: 650–64.

Camp, C. D. "Geriatrics," *Journal of the Michigan Medical Society* (1939), 38: 289–95.

Campbell, C. M. "Human Needs and Social Resources," in *Mental Health* (Moulton and Komora, eds.), Lancaster, Pa., Science Press, 1939, pp. 457–70.

Capps, Harry M. "Vocabulary Changes in Mental Deterioration," *Archives of Psychology* (March, 1940), No. 242, p. 80.

Carlson, A. J. "The Older Worker," *Scientific Monthly* (July, 1943), 57: 5–11.

Carrel, Alexis. "The Problem of the Prolongation of Life," *Proceedings of the Association of Life Insurance Presidents* (1937), p. 154.

Christian, Alice M., and Donald Paterson. "Growth of Vocabulary in Later Maturity," *Journal of Psychology* (1936), 1: 167–69.

Christian, H. A. "Some Limitations in Preventive Medicine," *Annals of Internal Medicine* (1939), 12: 1499–1506.

Cohn, A. "Old Age and Ageing from Point of View of Cardio-vascular System," *American Journal of Orthopsychiatry* (1940), 10: 43–55.

Collins, A. F. How to Ride Your Hobby. New York, Appleton-Century, 1935.

Collins, S. D. A General View of the Causes of Illness and Death at Specific Ages. Washington, U.S. Public Health Service, 1935. United States Public Health Reports, 50: 237–55.

Conover, Charlotte Reese. On Being Eighty. Yellow Springs, Ohio, Antioch Bookplate Co., 1941.

Conkey, F. "Adaptations of Fifty Men and Fifty Women to Old Age," *Journal of Home Economics* (1933), 2: 387–89.

Conrad, H. S. "General Information, Intelligence, and the Decline of Intelligence," *Journal of Applied Psychology* (1930), 14: 589–599.

—— "Measurement of Adult Intelligence and the Requisites for a General Intelligence," *Journal of Applied Psychology* (1930), 14: 589–599.

Conrad, H. S., H. E. Jones, and H. H. Hsiao. "Sex Differences in Mental Growth and Decline," *Journal of Educational Psychology* (1933), 24: 161–69.

Corwin, E. H. L. "Standards for Guidance of Institutional Convalescence," *Modern Hospital* (1925), 25: 144–45.

Courtenay, Charles. On Growing Old Gracefully. New York, Macmillan, 1936.

Cowdry, E. V. (ed.). Problems of Ageing; Biological and Medical Aspects. Baltimore, Williams & Wilkins, 2d ed. rev., 1942.

Cowdry, E. V. "We Grow Old," *Scientific Monthly* (Jan., 1940), 50: 51–58.

Crampton, C. W. "Physiological Age; a Fundamental Principle," *American Physical Education Review* (1908), 13: 141–54.

Critchley, M. "The Neurology of Old Age," *Lancet* (May 23, 1931), 220: 1119.

Currier, Andrew F. The Menopause. New York, D. Appleton and Co., 1897.

De Silva, Harry R. Driver Testing Results. Boston, Works Progress Administration of Massachusetts, Project No. 6246–12259, 1937.

—— "Age and Highway Accidents," *Scientific Monthly* (1938), 47: 536–46.

De Tarnovsky, G. "Surgery of the Aged; Indications and Contra-indications," *Surgical Clinics of North America* (1940), 20: 3–12.

Dietz, J. W. "An Experiment with Vocationally Handicapped Workers," *Personnel Journal* (1932), 10: 365–70.

Dill, D. B., and others. "Industrial Fatigue," *Journal of Industrial Hygiene and Toxicology* (1937), 18: 417–31.

Doll, Edgar A. Making the Most of Maturity. Boston, John Hancock Co., 1940. Life Conservation Series.

—— "Measurement of Social Maturity Applied to Older People," in *Mental Health in Later Maturity*, Supplement No. 168, U.S. Public Health Service Reports, Washington, D.C., 1943.

Douglas, R. J. "Male Climacteric: Its Diagnosis and Treatment," *Journal of Urology* (1941), 45: 404.

Dublin, L. I. "Statistical and Social Implications in the Problem of our Ageing Population," in *Medical Problems of Old Age*. Philadelphia, University of Pennsylvania Press, 1941.

Dublin, L. I., and A. J. Lotka. Length of Life. New York, Ronald Press, 1936.

Dublin, L. I., and H. H. Marks. "The Inheritance of Longevity; a Study Based upon Life Insurance Records," *Proceedings of the Association of Life Insurance Medical Directors of America* (1942), 28: 89–126.

Dutcher, Elizabeth. "Care of the Aged from the Point of View of the Public Agency," *The Family* (July, 1926).

Eisenstaedt, J. S. "Urologic Conditions in the Aged," *Medical Clinics of North America* (1940), 24: 157–64.

Elliott, G. L. Women after Forty; the Meaning of the Last Half of Life. New York, Henry Holt & Co., 1936.

Engelbach, W. "Relation of Endocrine Disorders to Senescence," *Bulletin of the New York Academy of Medicine* (1929), 2d ser., 5: 1–19.

Epstein, Abraham. Facing Old Age. New York, Alfred A. Knopf, 1922.

—— "New Developments in the Care of the Aged," *Hospital Social Service* (1926), 14: 21–27.

Etling, G. F. "Therapeutic Considerations in Psychoses of Old Age," *Psychiatric Quarterly* (1940), 14: 274–84.

Fitts, J. B. "Nutrition and Longevity," *Medical Times* (1941), 69: 459.

Folsom, Joseph K. The Family; Its Sociology and Social Psychiatry. New York, John Wiley & Sons, 1934.

Folsom, Joseph K. "Old Age as a Sociological Problem," *American Journal of Orthopsychiatry* (1940), 10: 30–42.

Fox, F. and others. Mental Hygiene and Old Age. New York, Family Welfare Association of America, 1937.

Franklin, Z. C. "Little-known Facts about Grandparents," *Parents Magazine* (1934), 9: 16–17.

Franz, S. I. "Rehabilitation and Reeducation—Physical, Mental, and Social," *Mental Hygiene* (1919), 3: 33–47.

Freeman, Frank N. "Intellectual Growth Based on Longitudinal Studies," *Bulletin of the School of Education, Indiana University* (Sept., 1938).

Freeman, J. T. "History of Geriatrics," *Annals of Medical History* (1938), 10: 324–35.

—— "Status of Geriatrics," *Pennsylvania Medical Journal* (1940), 43: 813–16.

Garrett, H. E., A. I. Bryan, and R. E. Perl. "The Age Factor in Mental Organization," *Archives of Psychology* (1935), No. 176.

Gavigan, A. J. "Care of Aged; Its Medical Aspects," *American Journal of Nursing* (1939), 39: 145–49.

Gilbert, Jeanne G. "Mental Efficiency in Senescence," *Archives of Psychology* (1935), No. 188: 1–44.

—— "Senescent Efficiency and Employability," *Journal of Applied Psychology* (1936), 20: 266–72.

—— "Memory Loss in Senescence," *Journal of Abnormal and Social Psychology* (Jan., 1941), 36: 73–86.

Goldfarb, W. "An Investigation of Reaction Time in Older Adults, and Its Relationship to Certain Observed Mental Test Patterns," Columbia University, *Teachers College, Contributions to Education* (1941): No. 831, pp. viii–76.

Goldstein, H. "Nursing the Aged," *Trained Nurse* (1941), 107: 257.

Grace, A. G. "The Reading Interests of Adults," *Journal of Educational Research* (1929), 19: 265–75.

Gray, W. S., and R. Munroe. The Reading Interests and Habits of Adults. New York, Macmillan, 1929.

Greenbie, M. L. Arts of Leisure. New York, McGraw-Hill Book Co., 1935.

Greifer, Julian L. "Time to Kill," *Recreation* (1937), 31: 345–48.

Greenwood, M., and J. O. Irwin. "Biostatistics of Senility," *Human Biology* (1939), 11: 1–23.

Grotjahn, M. "Psychoanalytic Investigation of a 71-year-old Man with Senile Dementia," *Psychoanalytic Quarterly* (1940), 9: 80–97.

Haas, Louis J. Occupational Therapy for the Mentally and Nervously Ill. Milwaukee, Bruce Publishing Co., 1925.

Hasley, H. C. Effect of Tobacco on Longevity. *Journal of Medicine* (1941), 22: 24.

Haggard, H. W., and L. A. Greenberg. Intellectual and Physical Efficiency. New Haven, Yale University Press, 1935.
Hall, G. Stanley. Senescence: the Last Half of Life. New York, Appleton, 1923.
Hambridge, G. Time to Live; Adventures in the Use of Leisure. New York, McGraw-Hill Book Co., 1933.
Hamilton, Gordon. "Case Work in Old Age Assistance," *The Family* (Feb., 1938).
Hanna, Joseph V. "Job Stability and Earning Power of Emotionally Maladjusted as Compared with Emotionally Adjusted Workers," *Journal of Abnormal and Social Psychology* (1935), 30: 144–63.
Harris, D. "Age and Occupational Factors in the Residential Propinquity of Marriage Partners," *Journal of Social Psychology* (1935), 6: 257–61.
Haworth, N. A., and E. M. Macdonald. The Theory of Occupational Therapy. London, Bailliere, Tindall & Cox, 1940.
Heidler, J. B., and H. C. Lehman. "Chronological Age and Productivity; Various Types of Literature," *English Journal* (1937), 27: 294–305.
Heiser, V. G. "Influence of Nutrition on Diseases of Middle and Old Age," *Scientific Monthly* (1939), 49: 304–10.
Helton, Roy. "Old People: a Rising National Problem," *Harpers* (Oct., 1939), 179: 449–59.
Henninger, J. M. "The Senile Sex Offender," *Mental Hygiene* (1939), 23: 436–44.
Hill, Ruth. "Social Case Work as Applied to Old Age Assistance," *The Family* (Oct., 1935).
—— "Understanding the Problems of Older People," *The Family* (Jan., 1938).
Hochhauser, W. "A Sheltered Workshop for the Tuberculous," *Occupational Therapy* (1932), 11: 185–93.
Hollingworth, H. L. Mental Growth and Decline. New York, Appleton, 1927.
Hollingworth, L. S. "Do Intellectually Gifted Children Grow toward Mediocrity in Stature?" *Pedagogical Seminary and Journal of Genetic Psychology* (1930), 37: 345–60.
Horn, W. S. "Geriatrics as a Modern Specialty," *Texas State Journal of Medicine* (1937), 33: 448.
—— "Diet in Old Age," *Medical Press* (1940), 203: 152–54.
Hoskins, R. G., H. M. Levene, and S. Bevin. "Relationship of Male Sex Hormone to Level of Bodily Vigor in Senility," *Endrocrinology* (1939), 25: 143–44.
Hubbell, R. A. "Men and Women Who Have Performed Distinctive Service after the Age of 74," *Wilson Bulletin* (1935), 9: 297–304.
Hudson and Van Gelde. Counselling the Handicapped. New York, National Tuberculosis Association, 1940.

Infeld, H. "The Aged in the Process of Ethnic Assimilation," *Sociometry* (1940), 3: 353–65.

"I Went to College at Fifty," *Forum* (Dec., 1939), 102: 284–86.

Jarrett, M. C. The Care of the Chronic Sick in Private Homes for the Aged in and near New York City. New York, Welfare Council, 1931. Research Bureau, Study 5.

——, "Chronically Ill and Aged; Standards for Care of These Patients," *Modern Hospital* (1938), 51: 45–47.

Johnson, M. "Doctors for Dotage," *Magazine Digest* (1940), 21: 27–29.

Jones, H. E., and H. S. Conrad. "The Growth and Decline of Intelligence," *Genetic Psychology Monographs* (1933), 13: 1–298.

Josselyn, D. W. Live Up to Yourself; How to Make the Most of Your Energy. New York, Longmans, Green, 1941.

Kahn, E., and L. W. Simmons. "Problems of Middle Age," *Yale Review* (1940), 29: 349–63.

Kardiner, A. "Psychological Factors in Old Age," in *Mental Hygiene in Old Age; a Symposium.* New York, Family Welfare Association of America, 1937.

Kaufman, M. R. "Old Age and Ageing; Psychoanalytic Point of View," *American Journal of Orthopsychiatry* (1940), 10: 74–84.

—— "Psychoanalysis in Late-Life Depressions," *Psychoanalytic Quarterly* (1937), 6: 308–35.

Kelley, N. H. "Study in Presbycousis; Auditory Loss with Increasing Age and Its Effect on Perception of Music and Speech," *Archives of Otolaryngology* (1939), 29: 506–13.

Knight, F. B., and H. Remmers. "Fluctuations in Mental Production When Motivation Is the Main Variable," *Journal of Applied Psychology* (1923), 7: 209–23.

Komarovsky, M. The Unemployed Man and His Family; the Effect of Unemployment upon the Status of the Man in Fifty-nine Families. New York, Dryden Press, 1940.

Kossoris, M. D. "Relation of Age to Industrial Injuries," *Monthly Labor Review* (1940), 17: 789–804.

Kounin, J. S. "Experimental Studies of Rigidity. I: The Measurement of Rigidity in Normal and Feeble-minded Persons," *Character and Personality* (1941), 9: 273–82.

Kubo, Yoshihide. "Mental and Physical Changes in Old Age," *Pedagogical Seminary and Journal of Genetic Psychology* (1938), 53: 101–8.

Kuhlen, R. G. "Social Change: a Neglected Factor in Psychological Studies of the Life Span," *School and Society* (1940), 52: 14–16.

Kurtz, Russell H. "Social Case Work in the National Program of Social Security," *The Family* (Oct., 1935).

Lambert, S. "Alcohol and Old Age," *Bulletin of the New York Academy of Medicine* (1928), 2d ser., 4: 1111.

Lampland, R. (ed.). Hobbies for Everybody. New York, Harper, 1934.

Landis, J. T. "What Is the Happiest Period in Life?" *School and Society* (1942), 55: 643–45.

Laplace, L. B., and J. J. Nicholson. "Prolonged Recumbency as a Contributory Cause of Death in Elderly Persons," *Journal of the American Medical Association* (Jan. 22, 1938), 110: 247–51.

Lawton, George. "After 65?" *Mental Hygiene* (July, 1941), 25, No. 3.

—— "Constructive Proposals for the Older Worker," *Personnel Journal* (Feb., 1940), 18: 300–308.

—— "A Discussion Group: Average Age 75," *Journal of Adult Education* (1939), 10: 387–95.

—— "Happiness in Old Age," *Mental Hygiene* (April, 1943), 27: 231–37.

—— "In Search of Old Age; Case Presentation of an 82-year-old Man," *Journal of Orthopsychiatry*, forthcoming.

—— "A Long-Range Research Program in the Psychology of Old Age and Aging," *Journal of Social Psychology* (1940), 12: 101–14.

—— "Mental Abilities at Senescence," *Journal of Applied Psychology* (Dec., 1938), 22: 607–19.

—— "Mental Hygiene at Senescence," *Mental Hygiene* (1939), 23: 257–67.

—— "Not Quite Heaven; the Story of the Colony for the Aged at Millville, N.J.," *Saturday Evening Post* (May 9, 1942).

—— "Old Age and Ageing; Present Status of Scientific Knowledge," *American Journal of Orthopsychiatry* (1940), 10: 27–29, 85–87.

—— "Possibilities for Psychologists in Work with the Aged," *Journal of Consulting Psychology* (March–April, 1942), 6: 89–91.

—— "Psychological Basis for Discrimination against Older Workers," in *Final Report of New York State Joint Legislative Committee on Discrimination in Employment of the Middle-Aged* (March, 1940).

—— "Psychological Guidance for Older Persons," in E. V. Cowdry, *Problems of Ageing*, 2d ed. rev., 1942.

Lawton, George (ed.). "Psychology and Later Maturity," A Symposium, in *American Journal of Orthopsychiatry*, forthcoming.

Leacock, S. "This Business of Growing Old," *New York Times Magazine* (Dec. 31, 1939).

Lehman, Harvey C. "The Creative Years: Best Books," *Scientific Monthly* (1937), 45: 65–75.

—— "The Creative Years: Medicine, Surgery, and Certain Related Fields," *Scientific Monthly* (1941), 52: 450–61.

—— "The Creative Years in Science and Literature," *Scientific Monthly* (1936), 43: 151–62.

—— "The Most Proficient Years at Sports and Games," *Research Quarterly, American Association of Health and Physical Education* (1938), 9: 3–19.

Lehman, Harvey C., and Walter S. Gamertsfelder. "Man's Creative Years in Philosophy," *Psychological Review* (July, 1942), 49: 319–43.

Levitt, G. "Electrocardiogram in the Aged; Study of 100 Men and Women over 70 with Apparently Normal Hearts," *American Heart Journal* (1939), 18: 692–96.

Lockwood, C. D. "Major Surgery in People of Advanced Age," *Surgical Clinics of North America* (1933), 13: 105–11.

"Longevity of American People," *Statistical Bulletin, Metropolitan Life Insurance Co.* (1938), 19: 5.

Lorge, Irving. "The Influence of the Test upon the Nature of Mental Decline as a Function of Age," *Journal of Educational Psychology* (Feb., 1936), 27: 100–110.

—— "Intellectual Changes during Maturity and Old Age," *Review of Educational Research* (Dec., 1941), 11: 553–61.

—— "Never Too Late to Learn," *Journal of the American Association of University Women* (Oct., 1937), 31: 27–32.

—— "Psychometry; Evaluation of Mental Status as Function of Mental Test," in symposium "Old Age and Aging," *American Journal of Orthopsychiatry* (1940), 10: 56–61.

—— "Psychological Bases for Adult Learning," *Teachers College Record* (Oct., 1939), 41: 4–12.

—— "Review of *Time and the Mind* by Harriet Babcock," in *Journal of Consulting Psychology* (Aug.–Sept., 1942), 6: 270.

McCay, C. M. "Diet and Ageing," *Journal of the American Dietetic Association* (1941), 17: 540.

Mackay, R. P. "The Psychoses of Old Age," *Medical Clinics of North America* (1940), 24: 93–104.

McKenzie, R. T. "Compensations at Seventy," *Transactions and Studies of the College of Physicians* (1938–39), 6: 271–81.

McLean, Francis H. "Opening the Door for the Aged," *The Family* (March, 1938).

McLester, J. S. "The Disabilities of Advancing Years; How to Meet Them," *New Orleans Medical and Surgical Journal* (1930–31), 83: 367–70.

Malamud, W. "Current Trends and Needs in Research on Problems of the Aged," *Diseases of the Nervous System* (1941), 2: 37–43.

Maller, J. B. "Mental Ability and Its Relation to Physical Health and Social Economic Status," *Psychological Clinic* (1933), 22: 101–7.

Maple, J. B. "Geriatrics," *Journal of the Indiana Medical Association* (1939), 32: 406–9.

Maranon, Gregorio. The Climacteric. St. Louis, C. V. Mosby Company, 1929.

Martin, Lillien J., and C. De Gruchy. Salvaging Old Age. New York, Macmillan, 1930.

—— Sweeping the Cobwebs. New York, Macmillan, 1933.

Mearns, Hughes. The Creative Adult. New York, Doubleday, Doran, 1940.

Mechnikov, I. The Prolongation of Life. New York, Putnams, 1908.

Mellum, H. J. "Employment of the Handicapped," *Occupational Therapy* (1926), 5: 335–42.

Mental Health in Later Maturity, Supplement No. 168 to the Public Health Reports, U.S. Public Health Service, Washington, D.C., 1942.

Mental Hygiene in Old Age, A Symposium. New York, Family Welfare Association of America, 1937.

Meyer, J. "Management of Diseases of Gastrointestinal Tract in Aged," *Medical Clinics of North America* (1940), 24: 9–21.

Miles, C. C. "Influence of Speed and Age on Intelligence Scores of Adults," *Journal of General Psychology* (1934), 10: 208–10.

Miles, Walter R. "Age and Human Ability," *Psychological Review* (1933), 40: 99–123.

—— "Age in Human Society," in *A Handbook of Social Psychology*, ed. by C. Murchison. Worcester, Mass., Clark University Press, 1935.

—— "The Maintenance of Our Mental Abilities," *Scientific Monthly* (1933), 34: 549–52.

—— "Measures of Certain Abilities throughout the Life Span," *Proceedings of the National Academy of Sciences* (1931), 17: 627–33.

—— "Psychological Aspects of Ageing," in E. V. Cowdry, *Problems of Ageing: Biological and Medical Aspects*, 2d ed., rev., 1942.

—— "Training, Practice, and Mental Longevity," *Science* (Jan., 1935), 81: 79–97.

Miles, Walter R., and C. C. Miles. "The Correlation of Intelligence Scores and Chronological Age from Early to Late Maturity," *American Journal of Psychology* (1932), 44: 44–78.

Morgan, A. F. "Vitamins and Senescence," *Scientific Monthly* (May, 1941), 52: 416–21.

Morgan, C. M. "The Attitudes and Adjustments of Recipients of Old Age Assistance in Upstate and Metropolitan New York," *Archives of Psychology* (1937), No. 214.

—— What Makes Old People Happy? *Survey* (Dec., 1935), 71: 360–61.

Morrow, Margaret I. "The Use of Therapeutic Techniques in Releasing Old-Age Tensions," *Social Work Technique* (March–April, 1937).

Mueller-Denham, A., and S. M. Robson. Internal Medicine in Old Age. Baltimore, Williams & Wilkins, 1942.

Myers, J. Q. "Family Doctor's Care of His Elderly Patients," *Southern Medicine and Surgery* (1938), 100: 278–80.

Nascher, I. L. Geriatrics. 2d ed., Philadelphia, Blakiston, 1916.

—— "The Institutional Care of the Aged," *Medical Review of Reviews* (1917), 23: 501–6.

National Recreation Association. The Leisure Hours of 5000 People. New York, National Recreation Association, 1935. (Mimeographed.)

Newman, B. M. "Must We Grow Old?" *Scientific American* (1938), 159: 285–88.

Oberndorf, Clarence P. "Sublimation in Occupational Therapy," *Occupational Therapy and Rehabilitation* (June, 1932), 11: 155–67.
Oberndorf, Clarence P., and A. Eisendorfer. "Anxiety in a Neurosis of Seventy Years' Standing," *Psychiatric Quarterly* (April, 1942), 16: 221–29.
Overholser, W. "Some Mental Problems of Ageing and Their Management," *Medical Annals of the District of Columbia* (1941), 10: 212.
Palmer, Dwight L., and John A. Brownell. "Influence of Age on Employment Opportunities," *Monthly Labor Review* (April, 1939), Series No. R. 889.
Pearl, Raymond. The Ancestry of the Long-Lived. Baltimore, Johns Hopkins Press, 1934.
—— "Harvey's Postmortem Examination of Thomas Parr (a Centenarian)," *Human Biology* (1931), 3: 138–42.
—— "Influence of Alcohol in the Duration of Life," *Proceedings of the National Academy of Sciences* (1934), 10: 231.
—— "The Search for Longevity," *Scientific Monthly* (May, 1938), 46: 462.
—— "Tobacco Smoking and Longevity," *Science* (1938), 87: 216.
Pearl, Raymond, and S. Greef. "Biology and Human Trends," *Journal of the Washington Academy of Sciences* (1935), 25: 253–72.
Pepper, O. H. P. "Principles of Diagnosis and Treatment of Disease in the Elderly," *Nebraska Medical Journal* (1939), 24: 401–6.
Peters, Iva L. "Rehabilitation Applied to Older Persons," *American Journal of Orthopsychiatry* (forthcoming).
Peterson, W. F., and H. H. Reese. "Psychotic and Somatic Interrelations," *Journal of the American Medical Association* (1940), 115: 1587–91.
Pettee, E. H. "Care of the Aged; Its Nursing Aspects," *American Journal of Nursing* (1939), 30: 150–55.
Piersol, George M., and Edward L. Bortz. "The Ageing Process; a Medico-Social Problem," *Annals of Internal Medicine* (Jan., 1939), 12: 964.
Pintner, R., J. Eisenson, and M. Stanton. The Psychology of the Physically Handicapped. New York, Crofts, 1941.
Pitkin, Walter B. Life Begins at Forty. New York, McGraw-Hill Book Co., 1932.
—— Careers after Forty. New York, McGraw-Hill Book Co., 1937.
Pollack, O. "The Criminality of Old Age," *Journal of Criminal Psychopathology* (1941), 3: 213–35.
Pressey, S. L., J. E. Janney, and R. G. Kuhlen. Life: a Psychological Survey. New York, Harpers, 1939.
"Problems of the Older Worker in the United States and Europe," *Monthly Labor Review* (Feb., 1939), Series No. R. 890.
Prosser, Charles A., and W. I. Hamilton. The Teacher and Old Age. Boston, Houghton Mifflin, 1913.

Prout, C. T., and A. V. Bourcier. "Mental Problems of Midlife," *New England Journal of Medicine* (1940), 223: 576–81.

Reznikoff, L. "Emotional Factors in the Rehabilitation of the Physically Disabled," *American Journal of Psychiatry* (1938), 94: 819–24.

Rhein, J. H. W., N. W. Winkelmann, and C. A. Patten. "Mental Conditions in the Aged," *Archives of Neurology and Psychiatry* (1928), 20: 329–35.

Robinson, G. W., Jr. "Acute Confusional States of Old Age; Their Interpretation and Treatment," *Southern Medical Journal* (1939, 32: 479–86.

—— "Psychiatric Geriatrics; Possibilities in Treatment of Mental States of Old Age," *Journal of the American Medical Association* (1941), 116: 2139.

Rothschild, D. "Pathologic Changes in Senile Psychoses and Their Psychobiologic Significance," *American Journal of Psychiatry* (Jan., 1937), 93: 757–88.

Rubinow, I. M. (ed.). "Care of the Aged," *Proceedings of the Deutsch Foundation Conference* (1931).

Ruch, Floyd L. "Adult Intelligence," in *Encyclopedia of Educational Research* (1941).

—— "Adult Learning," *Psychological Bulletin* (1933), 30: 387–414.

—— "The Differentative Effects of Age upon Human Learning," *Journal of General Psychology* (1934), 11: 261–86.

Ruger, Henry A., and Brenda Stoessiger. "Growth Curves of Certain Characteristics in Man (Males)," *Annals of Eugenics* (1927), 2: 76–110.

Schilder, Paul. "Psychiatric Aspects of Old Age and Ageing," *American Journal of Orthopsychiatry* (1940), 10: 62–72.

Schneider, D. M. "Medical Care for the Dependent Aged," *Public Health Nursing* (1937), 29: 452–57.

Schneider, Margaret G. More Security for Old Age. New York, Twentieth Century Fund, 1937.

Schooley, M. "Personality Resemblance among Married Couples," *Journal of Abnormal and Social Psychology* (1936), 31: 340–47.

Scott, Colin. "Old Age and Death," *American Journal of Psychology* (1896), 8: 67–122.

Seidenfeld, Morton A. "Measuring Mental Competence in the Senile," *American Journal of Orthopsychiatry* (forthcoming).

Shakow, David. "The Memory Function in Psychoses of the Aged," in Symposium on Problems of the Aged, *Diseases of the Nervous System* (1941), 2: 3–8.

Shakow, David, and Rosalie Goldman. "The Effect of Age on the Stanford-Binet Vocabulary Score of Adults," *Journal of Educational Psychology* (April, 1938), 29: 241–56.

Shipley, Walter C. "A Self-Administering Scale for Measuring Intellectual Impairment and Deterioration," *Journal of Psychology* (April, 1940).

Simms, H. S. "Physiological Alterations as Cause of Senile Debility and Senile Mortality," *Science* (1940), 91: 7–9.

Simon, B., and S. H. Kaufman. "Psychiatric Problems of the Aged," *Diseases of the Nervous System* (1941), 2: 62–65.

Simpson, Lola Jean. "A Place in the Sun," *Journal of Adult Education* (April, 1932).

Smith, Elliott Dunlap. What Are the Psychological Factors of the Obsolescence of Workers in Middle Age? New York, American Management Association, 1931. Personnel Series, No. 9.

Smith, Nicholas. Masters of Old Age. Milwaukee, The Young Churchman Co., 1905.

Sorenson, Herbert. Adult Abilities; a Study of University Extension Students. Minneapolis, University of Minnesota Press, 1938.

—— "Adult Ages as a Factor in Learning," *Journal of Educational Psychology* (1930), 21: 451–59.

—— "Mental Ability over a Wide Range of Adult Ages," *Journal of Applied Psychology* (1933), 17: 729–41.

Stevens, A. F., Jr. "Accidents of Older Workers; Relation of Age to Extent of Disability," *Personnel Journal* (1934), 8: 138–45.

Stewart, Maxwell S. Pensions after Sixty. Public Affairs Pamphlets, No. 46 (1940).

Stieglitz, Edward J. Abnormal Arterial Tension. New York, National Medical Book Co., 1935.

—— "Ageing as an Industrial Health Program," *Journal of the American Medical Association* (March 29, 1941), 116: 1383–87.

—— "Investigation in Gerontology," *Diseases of the Nervous System* (1941), 2: 74–75.

—— "The Potentialities of Preventive Geriatrics," *New England Journal of Medicine* (Aug. 14, 1941), 225: 247–54.

—— Report of a Survey of Active Studies in Gerontology. Washington, Unit on Gerontology, Division of Chemotherapy, National Institute of Health, 1942.

—— "Wise Investment of Leisure," *Scientific Monthly* (1940), 51: 147.

Stieglitz, Edward J. (ed.). Geriatric Medicine. Philadelphia, W. B. Saunders Co., 1943.

Strauss, Clifford A. "Grandma Made Johnny Delinquent," *American Journal of Orthopsychiatry* (April, 1943), 8: 343–46.

Strong, E. K., Jr. Change of Interests with Age. Stanford University, Stanford University Press, 1931.

Stroud, J. B., and Ruth Maul. "The Influence of Age on Learning and Retention of Poetry and Nonsense Syllables," *Pedagogical Seminary and Journal of Genetic Psychology* (1933), 42: 242–50.

Study, A, of Occupations at Which 6,097 Physically Disabled Persons

Are Employed after Being Vocationally Rehabilitated, *Bulletin of the Federal Board of Vocational Education* (Jan., 1925), No. 96.
Symonds, P. M. "Happiness as Related to Problems and Interests," *Journal of Educational Psychology* (1937), 28: 290–94.
—— "Life Problems and Interests of Adults," *Teachers College Record* (1936), 38: 144–51.
Taub, S. J. "Treatment of Allergic Diseases of the Aged," *Medical Clinics of North America* (1940), 24: 149–56.
Thewlis, M. W. Care of the Aged (Geriatrics). 4th ed. St. Louis, C. V. Mosby Co., 1942.
Thompson, W. O. "Endocrine Problems in Later Life," *Medical Clinics of North America* (1940), 24: 79–91.
Thompson, Warren S., and P. K. Whelpton. Population Trends in the United States. New York, McGraw-Hill Book Co., 1933.
Thorndike, E. L., and others. Adult Learning. New York, Macmillan, 1928.
Tilney, F. "The Ageing of the Human Brain," *Bulletin of the New York Academy of Medicine*, 2d series (1928), 4: 1125–43.
Tuohy, E. L. "Geriatrics in Relation to Adequate Energy-Producing and Protective Diet," *Journal of the American Medical Association* (1940), 114: 223–27.
Tyson, W. J. "The Danger of Putting Old People to Bed," *Clinical Journal* (1923), 52: 383–407.
Vollmer, Hermann. "The Grandmother: a Problem in Child-Rearing," *American Journal of Orthopsychiatry* (July, 1937), 7: 378–82.
Voronoff, Serge. The Conquest of Life. New York, Brentano, 1928.
Vorse, Mary Heaton. Autobiography of an Elderly Woman. Boston, Houghton, Mifflin, 1911.
Walsh, J. J. "The Enigma of Long Life," *International Clinics* (1932), 4: 14–25.
Warner, Frances L. "How to be Loved When Old," *Atlantic Monthly* (Feb., 1942).
Warthin, A. S. Old Age, the Major Involution; the Physiology and Pathology of the Aging Process. New York, Hoeber, 1929.
Watters, T. A. "Nervous and Mental Aspects of Old Age," *New Orleans Medical and Surgical Journal* (1940), 93: 187–93.
Webb, Gerald B. "Climate and the Aged," *Bulletin of the New York Academy of Medicine* (1928), 2d series, 4: 1213.
Weber, Sir Herman. On Longevity and Prolongation of Life. 5th ed. London, Macmillan, 1919.
Wechsler, David. The Measurement of Adult Intelligence. 2d ed., rev., Baltimore, Williams & Wilkins, 1941.
—— The Range of Human Capacities, Baltimore, Williams & Wilkins, 1935.
Weisenburg, T. H., Anne Roe, and K. S. McBride. Adult Intelligence. New York, Commonwealth Fund, 1936.

Williams, C. "Opportunities for Improving the Health of the Aged in the Administration of the Massachusetts Old Age Assistance Law," *New England Medical and Surgical Journal* (1931), 205: 955–63.

Williams, Leonard. Middle Age and Old Age. London, Oxford University Press, 1925.

Willius, F. A. "Cardiac Clinics: Talks on the Adjustment of Man to Advancing Years of Life," *Proceedings of Staff Meetings, Mayo Clinic* (1939), 14: 41–43.

—— "Cardiac Clinics; Recreational Exercise in the Advancing Years of Life," *Proceedings of Staff Meetings, Mayo Clinic* (1942), 17: 6.

Wissler, C. "Age Changes in Anthropological Characters in Childhood and Adult Life," *Proceedings of the American Philosophical Society* (1927), 66: 431–38.

Witty, P. A. "Reading Interests and Habits of 500 Adults," *Education* (1932), 52: 554–62.

Worcester, Alfred. The Care of the Aged, the Dying, and the Dead. Springfield, Ill., Charles C. Thomas, 1935.

Yacorzynski, G. Y. "An Evaluation of the Postulates Underlying the Babcock Deterioration Test," *Psychological Review* (1941), 48: 261–67.

Young, T. E. On Centenarians and the Duration of the Human Race. London, C. & E. Layton, 1899.

INDEX

Bei Fragen zur Produktsicherheit wenden Sie sich bitte an:
If you have any questions regarding product safety,
please contact:

Walter de Gruyter GmbH
Genthiner Straße 13
10785 Berlin
productsafety@degruyterbrill.com